$$\mathcal{E} \frac{1}{\sqrt{1-u^2}} = \frac{2}{\sqrt{-u^2}\sqrt{1-v^2}}$$

$$\mathcal{E} \frac{u_i}{\sqrt{1-u^2}} = \frac{v_i}{\sqrt{1-u^2}\sqrt{1-v^2}}$$

$$\text{Hyp.} \quad \mathcal{E}\mathcal{I}_i = \mathcal{E}\overline{\mathcal{I}}_i$$

$$\mathcal{E}\ddot{\mathcal{E}} = \mathcal{E}\overline{\overline{\mathcal{E}}}\mathcal{L}$$

$$\mathcal{I}_i = m\, u_i \, \mathcal{F}(u)$$

$$\mathcal{E} = \mathcal{E}_i + m\, \mathcal{G}(u)$$

Albert Einstein

Books for children by William Wise

ALBERT EINSTEIN: Citizen of the World
SILVERSMITH OF OLD NEW YORK: Myer Myers
JONATHAN BLAKE:
The Life and Times of a Very Young Man

ALBERT EINSTEIN

Citizen of the World

WILLIAM WISE

illustrated by SIMON JERUCHIM

JEWISH PUBLICATION SOCIETY

Author's Note

I wish to thank Professor Peter G. Bergmann of Syracuse University and Professor John A. Wheeler of Princeton University for their kindness in answering certain technical questions, and to thank especially Mr. Leonard Sarason for his time and help during my efforts to understand something of the scientific problems which played such a paramount part in Albert Einstein's life.

Invaluable material for this book was provided by Dr. Einstein's published letters, speeches, and autobiographical writings. In addition, several biographies of Dr. Einstein were also extremely helpful. Grateful acknowledgment is made to Alfred A. Knopf, Inc., for permission to use brief excerpts from *Einstein, His Life and Times*, by Philipp Frank, translated by George Rosen. Very useful material was also found in *The Drama of Albert Einstein*, by Antonina Vallentin, (Doubleday), and in *Ideas and Opinions*, an anthology of Dr. Einstein's letters, speeches, and other material, published by Crown.

Books that were also of substantial help to the author were: *The Universe and Dr. Einstein*, by Lincoln Barnett (New American Library), *The Germans: Double History of a Nation*, by Emil Ludwig (Atlantic-Little, Brown), *Germany*, by George Peabody Gooch (Scribner), and *Albert Einstein: A Biographical Portrait*, by Anton Reiser (Albert and Charles Boni).

Albert Einstein

Outside in the street, a large crowd had gathered along the curb. A parade was coming, and the people of Munich, like most Germans in the 1880's, greatly enjoyed watching the soldiers and listening to the music of a military band.

Pauline Einstein, a pretty young woman, stood at the window of her suburban house and looked down at the crowd. A small, dark-haired boy stood on tiptoe beside her. "Albert," she said, "there's going to be a parade. I'll hold you and you can watch it too."

She picked Albert up and held him so that his feet rested on the window ledge, and together they watched the start of the parade. First the band came by, trumpets blaring, fifes shrieking, and drums loudly beating out the time. As the band passed below, the window panes in the room shook with the noise.

Then the cavalry troops rode past on their beautiful horses. They were followed by the foot soldiers, marching in perfect step, company after company. Their rifles stuck up stiffly above their shoulders, their leather boots made a cracking sound on the cobblestone street, their spiked helmets gleamed in the afternoon sun.

"Some day," Pauline Einstein said, thinking he would be pleased at the idea, "you will be a soldier too, Albert." She was surprised to feel him tremble, and to see the tears start down his cheeks.

"I hate . . . the soldiers," he said, speaking in the hesitant way that he often did. "I don't ever want to be a soldier." And she could only calm him by promising that he wouldn't have to become one unless he chose to when he was older.

It was puzzling, she thought later, for a boy to hate soldiers as Albert hated them. But then, Albert had always been a puzzling child—almost from the first.

He had been born four years before, on the 14th of March, 1879, in the south German city of Ulm. A year later, the Einstein family had left Ulm and moved to Munich, the capital of Bavaria.

As the months passed, Pauline and her husband, Hermann Einstein, had begun to worry about their son. They noticed that other children in the neighborhood—much younger children—could talk quite well, while Albert still couldn't speak a single word.

They went to the best doctors in Munich, and were assured that Albert was a perfectly healthy, normal child. And in time, of course, he finally did begin to talk like other children. Yet even now, they continued to worry about him. For the older he grew, the more clear it became that there was something unusual about this shy, soft-spoken little boy of theirs.

Often Albert's parents compared him with his sister, Maya, who was two years younger than he was. Then they thought to themselves: how different our two children are. Maya is always laughing and singing. She chatters from morning till night. She plays games with her dolls, games that she makes up herself. She is exactly what a little girl is supposed to be. But Albert—he hardly ever laughs or sings. He never says one word more than necessary. He doesn't like games. He's so solemn, so grave—what odd ideas must pass through his mind. If only he were older and could tell us about them, maybe we would understand what kind of child he really is.

Albert didn't care for the ordinary toys that most children love, but one evening he received a toy that delighted him as nothing ever had before. Uncle Rudy, Hermann's brother, gave it to Albert before supper. Drawing a round object out of a small cardboard box, he placed it in Albert's hand. "It's a compass," he said. "The needle points to North. No matter how far you turn the compass itself, the needle will always point in the same direction."

Albert stared at the compass, completely fascinated.

His family looked at him with surprise. They had never seen such color in his cheeks, such delight sparkling in his eyes. His whole being was filled with excitement, his face with wonder.

"But why does the needle always point the same way?" he said. "I can't see what makes it do that?"

Uncle Rudy laughed, and told the eager child that the needle was controlled by something called magnetism. An invisible force, he explained, which exists everywhere but which nobody can see.

Albert's parents were pleased at their son's interest in the toy magnet. For once, they felt, he'd forgotten himself, he was talking and smiling without shyness—exactly the way that Maya did when they gave her a new doll. And what an extraordinary toy for a child to be so interested in. "I think he will grow up to be an engineer," Hermann Einstein said, turning to Uncle Rudy. "An electrical engineer like you."

"Or he'll be a professor," said Albert's mother. "Do look at him. He hasn't taken his eyes away from the compass since you gave it to him, Rudy. Of course that's what he'll be, a professor in one of our famous universities."

She smiled to herself. It relieved her anxiety a little to see in Albert these first signs of unusual intelligence. Perhaps, she thought, he will turn out all right. Perhaps my worrying has been needless. Yes, from now on, the worst is over for Albert.

But the worst was really only beginning. Soon, he had to attend school, and school proved one of the greatest torments of his life. Often his marks were poor. He was called a lazy student, a stupid, or an indifferent one. His schoolteachers never recognized his incredible gifts, or even remembered, in later years, that they had once taught him in their classes.

Albert did poorly at school for several reasons. One reason was that he felt a deep, instinctive resentment against the cruelty of his teachers. In primary school, which he entered at six, the boys were shouted at and humiliated. Many times they were beaten. In class, when they were called on to answer questions, they were supposed to leap to their feet, stand rigid as soldiers, and snap out the required information like machines. Albert hated this military atmosphere. He longed for the day when he would be old enough to escape to a less brutal world.

Another reason why he did poorly in school was that he was often bored there. In the secondary school, called a "gymnasium," which he entered at ten, no effort was made to encourage the students to think for themselves. They were not even allowed to raise their hands to ask questions.

Most of the school day they spent memorizing the various rules of Latin and Greek grammar. Why, Albert thought, were Latin and Greek grammar so important? Why was so much time spent on them? If certain students were interested in other subjects, why, at least part of the day, couldn't they study what did interest them? But when he tried to explain these ideas to his teachers, they ignored him, or said that he was showing off, he was a disturbing element, a troublemaker.

Without being aware of it himself, Albert had begun a lifelong struggle against authority. Against the kind of blind authority which says, "We know what is true, what is right, what is best for you. We are your teachers, your rulers. You must think as we tell you to think. You must obey."

Even as a child, Albert could never readily submit to this kind of authority. He had to think his own thoughts, to try to see the world through his own eyes. And the rules of a German school, which said, "You are not free to think"—these rules he hated with all his strength.

During his early years, though, life did have a brighter side for Albert. At home, he lived in surroundings that were quite different from those at school. His parents were well-educated, middle-class Jews, who enjoyed spending their leisure time reading books, playing or listening to music, dining with their friends. There was never any haste to their lives, family quarrels were infrequent, and Albert, a quiet, peaceful boy, was left more and more to his own pursuits.

As he grew older, he spent many hours in his father's library. Hermann Einstein was a businessman—he owned a small factory outside Munich, where electrical equipment was manufactured—but he was a man with other interests besides business affairs. He read the German classics, and especially enjoyed the poems of Heine and Schiller, and soon Albert was reading these German poets too.

Albert's mother played the piano very well. Often the Einstein house would be filled with music, especially in the evenings, when one or another of the engineers from the factory would join her to play some of Beethoven's or Schubert's chamber music.

She insisted that Albert learn to play the violin. He began taking lessons when he was six, but until he was thirteen or fourteen, he disliked practicing almost as much as he disliked going to school. He did enjoy listening to his mother or to any skilled musician, but until he finally became more expert himself, he detested the groans and shrieks that came out of the violin when he practiced upstairs in his room. Still, he continued with his lessons, and when he was older, playing music became one of the few pleasures he knew outside of his work.

Albert's parents were kindly, easygoing people, but

neither of them was outstandingly gifted intellectually, nor did either of them have a scientific turn of mind. It was Uncle Rudy, a trained engineer, who did the most to stimulate Albert's natural interest in science and mathematics. When Albert began to study algebra, Uncle Rudy told him, "Algebra is really great fun. It's like hunting a mysterious animal—we call the animal 'x'—until we track him down, and capture him, and find out what he really is."

During the winter months, the weather was usually cold and damp, and the city of Munich seemed a gloomy place to Albert. In the summer, though, the Einsteins often went for outings in the country, and Albert particularly enjoyed these holiday excursions. His mother and father would sit in the front of the carriage and he and Maya would sit in the back, then off they would start, driving farther and farther along the beautiful country roads. Soon the gloom and darkness of the city had been left behind them. The air was filled with the sharp scent of pine trees. Great mountains rose in the distance. The sun glowed brightly on the fresh, green meadows.

Sometimes, for lunch, they would stop at a country inn and Albert would eat sausages and egg noodles, famous Bavarian dishes that were his favorites. Other times, the Einsteins joined friends and relatives and held a picnic beside the banks of the Isar River, or along the wooded shores of one of the lovely lakes that dotted the countryside.

On several of these picnics, Elsa Einstein, one of Albert's many cousins, was there with her parents. She was Maya's age and the two girls played together. Albert paid scant attention to Elsa—girls were not much to his taste just then—but years later he would remember these picnics with Elsa, and the memory would lead to a very important event in his life.

Albert had other cousins, who lived in Italy, and who came to Munich several times to visit. These Italian cousins lived in Genoa, and when they described their native city, the warm climate, the sunlight, the friendly people, Albert's imagination was stirred by what they told him. He felt that perhaps he would like Italy more than his own country, and wondered if some day he might have a chance to see it and to judge for himself.

After the Einsteins had been in Munich for five years, Hermann Einstein bought a new house for his family. Behind the house there was a small garden, where Albert loved to spend his free time when the weather was pleasant. Here everything was peaceful and still. He could watch the grass, the insects, the flowers, how they grew each year, how they died, how they were reborn the following spring. So much of Nature was filled with mystery. Yet something in Albert's mind told him that

much of what he saw was controlled by fixed and un-
changing laws which a person could understand if he
tried hard enough. Laws that would reveal a beautiful
sense of order, if they *were* understood.

God was in all of Nature—this, Albert came to believe at an early age. His study of the Bible led him to
believe so. In the Proverbs of Solomon he had read
these words many times: "The Lord by wisdom founded
the earth; by understanding He established the heavens.
By his knowledge the depths were broken up, and the
skies drop down the dew."

He had read too: "Happy is the man that findeth wisdom, and the man that obtaineth understanding. For the
merchandise of it is better than the merchandise of sil-
ver, and the gain thereof than fine gold."

Wisdom and understanding—these the Bible spoke
of as fitting goals for a man, and from the beginning Albert sensed that they would eventually become his own.

While still a child, he felt strongly drawn to his religion. He was taught that he was a Jew, and never afterward, though his beliefs underwent several changes,
denied that he was anything but a Jew.

When he read of the dietary laws prescribed in the
Bible, and found that they were not followed in his own
home, he was greatly distressed. His parents, though,
were lukewarm in their attitude to their religion. Like
many Jewish people who lived in Germany at the end
of the nineteenth century, the Einsteins had given up

most religious observances; they believed that they were more German than anything else, and that there was little reason for them to remain faithful to their religion.

Still, they did keep some of the older traditions, and one of these was the custom of inviting a poor Jewish student to their home each Thursday for dinner. One young medical student told Albert about a series of scientific books that had been written by a man named Aaron Bernstein. These books were written expressly for young people, and Albert, when he found one, was so taken with it that he soon persuaded his parents to buy him the entire series.

Some of the books in the series dealt with plants and animals, how they had developed millions of years ago, how they had changed through the ages, how the lives of different living things depended on each other. Some of the books were devoted to astronomy, to the stars and planets and meteors, to our own solar system. Some talked of the earth, the oceans, the formation of the continents, weather and climate and their effect on human life.

Albert read and reread each book in the series from cover to cover. Nature—the mysterious laws of Nature—here, it seemed to him, was an endless field for speculation. So many questions that had to be asked, so many answers that had to be discovered. And when the answers finally were discovered, what satisfaction to understand more about this universe of ours.

Then one day, when Albert was twelve, Uncle Rudy brought him another present. It was a book that was quite unlike any book that he had seen. It was devoted to the geometry of Euclid, and Albert raced through its pages with all the haste of a starving man devouring a banquet. His mind seemed to take flight, to soar beyond his surroundings into a world he had never known to exist.

His parents noticed his intense interest in the geometry book. They thought of his latest report card—he was still getting poor grades in most of his subjects—and they frowned with bewilderment. Obviously Albert *was* intelligent—why, then, did he not do better in school?

"One day he *will* do better," Hermann Einstein said, for he was an optimistic man who hated unpleasantness and who believed in looking on the cheerful side of every question.

"Well, I hope you're right," Pauline Einstein said with a sigh. "Nothing could please me more than to see Albert begin to find himself. He daydreams so much. I wish he could learn to settle down and spend more time on his schoolwork."

"He'll settle down soon enough," Hermann Einstein said. "Anyone as clever as Albert can turn around when he makes up his mind to it, and sweep aside everything that stands in his way. Tomorrow, the next day—wait and see. This geometry could be just what he needs to get him started."

Albert's father was mistaken, though. Albert had found the first dim clue to his future, but it would be a number of years before his troubles in school would be over. And it would be still longer before his parents, or anyone else, understood what Albert really was— not the lazy student, the vacant, idle dreamer they imagined—but a genius, whose work was destined to be known and honored in every civilized country in the world.

2

During his teens, life held many troubles for Albert. He knew loneliness and bitter disappointment. He experienced doubts about himself and about the world around him, and in time he became a rebel, at odds with the very country in which he had been born.

But he was fortunate in one respect—his parents were tolerant and intelligent people.

They did not understand their son. Many of his ideas were different from theirs. Many of his interests meant nothing to them. All during his teens he continued to worry and puzzle them, but they never tried to change him, or force him to act in ways that were contrary to his nature. They permitted him to follow his own path as much as they could, sensing that he was that one boy in a thousand who needs such freedom.

His teachers were less tolerant. Albert could rarely please them. They said he didn't prepare his homework, except in science and mathematics, and gave him poor grades, year after year. In science and mathematics, though, his teachers complained that he did too much homework—and asked too many questions. He knew more than he was supposed to know. Often, he knew more than they did.

One afternoon, his science teacher took Albert aside. "What were you trying to do today?" he said. "Those questions of yours. Did you want to upset my other students?"

"I only wanted to know the truth," Albert said, not understanding the painful embarrassment he had caused his teacher, by exposing his teacher's ignorance.

"Well, from now on you will not ask any more questions! Nobody can tell you the answers anyway—so please leave me and the rest of my class in peace!"

As he grew older, Albert slowly came to sense what his life interest would be, and he began to form a very ambitious plan for the future. What he felt he had to do was this: to study higher mathematics and the most advanced physics, so that one day, with the knowledge gained from these efforts, he would be able to examine for himself the ultimate physical laws that govern the universe. He wanted to explore with his mind the entire realm of physical matter, from the tiniest atom to the gigantic stars that rush through distant space. He wanted to learn how to understand such abstract and difficult questions as the nature of time and energy and motion, and to the understanding of these questions he planned to devote his life.

His interests were not limited, though, to questions of mathematics and science. The everyday world in which he lived concerned him, too—and often upset him deeply.

He hated the snobbishness of his teachers. They judged whether a student was rich or poor by the clothes he wore, and if he was rich they treated him politely, with respect.

Poor students were not so fortunate. They had no place to escape their misery—they were ill-treated in school and returned each night to the poverty and squalor of the slums. Sometimes, after leaving school in the afternoon, Albert felt ashamed of his own good luck in having such a pleasant, comfortable home to come back to.

He also thought a great deal about his country. For fifteen years he had lived in Germany. Yet with each passing day he realized more clearly how many things were wrong with the German nation, and how many of his own thoughts and feelings were antagonistic to those of his schoolmates, his family, and the majority of German citizens.

To understand why Albert felt that he was al-

most an alien in his own country, one must understand
something of what Germany was like at the end of the
nineteenth century.

She was a new nation. Indeed, until 1871 there had
been no Germany at all. Before that, for centuries, there
had been dozens of separate little German states, each
with its own prince and ruling family, each quarreling
jealously with its neighbors, each concerned only with
its own private affairs.

Then, in the north, a new power arose, the power of
Prussia. A confederation of German states was formed,
under Prussian leadership. Within eight years, three
wars were fought, each planned and directed by the
Prussian diplomat and statesman, Otto von Bismarck,
known afterward in history as "The Iron Chancellor."

First, there was the war with Denmark in 1864, then
the Seven Weeks' War with Austria in 1866, and finally
the Franco-Prussian War of 1870 with France. In all
three, Prussia and her allies were victorious. As a result of these victories, William I of Prussia was crowned
Emperor of Germany in 1871, and Germany became
not only a unified nation, but the most powerful on the
continent of Europe.

The influence of the Prussians on the rest of the German people soon grew very strong. This became clear
even in Bavaria, where Albert and his family lived.
Though Bavaria and Prussia had long been rivals, after

1871 Prussian manners and customs became more and more popular among the Bavarians.

Prussia, then, began to set its stamp on all of Germany. And Prussia was ruled by the "Junkers," a class of aristocrats who believed in war and conquest.

But what of the majority of Germans, who were neither aristocrats nor Prussians—why were they willing to accept without a struggle a military regime and a Prussian king? The answer is simple: they were accustomed to being ruled by kings and princes, and the stronger a king was, the more ready they were to accept him as their rightful leader.

The Germans had never known democracy and had few democratic traditions. They had little experience or training in personal or political independence. Many Germans held that obedience to authority was the greatest civic virtue—blind obedience.

This was one of the chief reasons why Albert so often felt himself set apart from the people he knew. He passionately believed that no authority on earth could rightfully demand such obedience. To obey without thought was to be a slave. A man wasn't free if he couldn't think for himself—and to Albert, such freedom was the same as breathing.

Albert also felt himself set apart because no one he talked with seemed in the least dismayed by the rising tide of Prussian militarism. As he listened to his family, to his family's friends, he had the feeling that all of them were perfectly willing to see their country become an armed camp. His schoolmates were willing, even eager, to serve in the Army and to kill their fellow men if necessary, "for the glory of the Fatherland."

Everywhere that he turned, he found fresh signs of this militaristic state of mind. In the magazines and newspapers that were delivered to the Einstein home, the Army was praised without question. Retired officers wrote of Germany's new greatness, her strength, and her need for African colonies. Speeches by members of a political War Party were printed, speeches which said that if the other nations of Europe stood in Germany's way, Germany should fight and conquer and take what she wanted.

In Munich, on holidays, there were numerous parades, and the sight of marching men still distressed Albert greatly. He felt an instinctive hatred of all uniforms —the symbols, to him, of men who were no longer men, but the debased servants of a cruel and dull-witted regime.

We Germans—what can be wrong with us? he often thought. What other people, throughout its history, has taken such *delight* in obedience, in following the commands of those in authority? Our schools—are other nations' schools like ours? Do all the teachers in the world try to turn their students into young soldiers —or only German teachers? Why, even our Emperor is not like the English king or the French president. When our Emperor's picture is taken, he is always wearing a uniform with a row of medals across his chest. Does the poor man have no other clothes to wear *except* a uniform?

Yet everyone that Albert knew seemed to admire William II, the newly crowned Emperor of Germany, grandson of the first Emperor. Everyone admired so many things that Albert detested . . . and he began to wonder for the first time if it were really possible for someone like himself to remain a citizen of Germany . . . or whether there might not be some other course open to him in the future?

By now he was almost sixteen. He had grown up to be a stocky, rather pleasant-looking youth, with a round, gentle face, and curly dark hair. He did have a way of becoming absent-minded when he was deep in thought, but despite this odd habit, his mother and father were sure that he was happier than he had been as a child.

He was less shy and withdrawn, he smiled more often, and, when he was with people he was accustomed to, delighted in telling jokes and funny stories. Then his eyes would twinkle good humoredly and the people around him would feel that even though he was "dreamy," a bit "different," he was still a very agreeable companion to pass the time with.

Life in Munich went on peacefully for Albert, as though nothing would ever change. At school, he received the highest possible grades in mathematics and physics, and almost the lowest in his other subjects. At home, having finally mastered something of the art of the violin, he began to play for his own enjoyment. He discovered the music of Mozart, the most beautiful music in the world he decided, an opinion that he held to the end of his life.

For some months, though, a shadow had been hanging over the Einstein household, and now it was no longer possible to ignore it. Hermann Einstein had long been in serious financial trouble. He owed money everywhere. Usually, if he spoke of his affairs at all, he said to Albert's mother, "Things will work out, Pauline. The business will take a turn for the better."

But by the summer of 1895, there was no longer any hope that things would improve. He had only one way of paying his debts. He had to sell the factory. Before long he was forced to offer the house for sale, too, the pretty house where all of them had lived for almost ten years. When the house had been sold and his debts paid, there was no money left. Hermann Einstein was a bankrupt.

Hurried letters were sent to uncles and cousins; family conferences were held, and finally, with money borrowed from relatives who were quite wealthy, Albert's parents left Germany, taking Maya with them. Albert's father planned to try his luck in Italy, to build or rent a factory there. Perhaps around Milan, where there were many skilled workers to be hired.

Almost overnight, Albert found himself alone. He was to remain in Munich for a year, in order to finish high school and earn his diploma. But Munich seemed a terrible place to him, once his mother and father and sister had gone. He moved into a rooming house. He ate his meals with strangers. He was not permitted to play his violin in his room, and he had no other place to play it. He had no garden where he could sit and read. The only people in the world he loved were living hundreds of miles away.

Many nights he felt too depressed to study. It seemed to rain every day during the fall; it seemed to snow every day during the winter. Cheerful letters came from Italy, from his parents and Maya, saying how warm the climate was, and what a pleasant house they had just rented in Milan.

Albert grew more depressed. Finally he decided that he couldn't bear to stay in Munich any longer.

An idea came to him. At first he was too ashamed to act on it. He knew it was dishonest, it involved telling lies, and he hated lies of any kind. He had never been able to tell them as a child, not even to save himself from punishment. But as week followed lonely week, he grew more desperate. He decided to act on his idea.

One cold, gray morning, instead of setting off for school, he put on his hat and coat and muffler, and went to see the Einsteins' family doctor, who was also a friend of his parents. He explained how miserable he was in Munich, and asked the doctor to certify that he was sick—to say that he was on the verge of a nervous breakdown—so that he could leave school and join his family in Italy.

The doctor was touched by Albert's sad expression. He saw that Albert had lost a good deal of weight. It was even possible that he might come down with a serious illness if he were left alone in the city much longer. So the doctor, who had a soft heart, wrote a letter saying that Albert had been sick lately, and that he should be excused from schoolwork for the rest of the year in order to regain his health. Albert stammered his thanks, his face radiant. Then he hurried to school and presented the doctor's letter to the principal.

Albert knew that by leaving before the end of the term, he would lose his chance of graduating from the "gymnasium" and of receiving his high school diploma. He also knew that he would need a diploma in order to enter college. So he asked his science and mathematics teachers for the next best thing—letters describing the advance work he had done in their subjects, as proof of his ability to undertake studies on the college level.

He was given these letters a week later, and with them, an unpleasant surprise. The school principal said, yes, it would be a good idea if Albert left school, but he didn't say a word about the doctor's letter or about Albert's supposed ill health.

Instead, he told Albert that several of his teachers had reported that he was a troublemaker, he was insubordinate, he tried to undermine their authority in the classroom.

Good riddance to young Einstein was *their* opinion, and the principal hinted that he agreed with them, and that he was far from sorry to see Albert's name dropped from the school roll.

So Albert left the "gymnasium" under a cloud, bewildered by the charges made against him, for he did not realize how much his indifference had insulted some of his teachers, and how much his brilliance had embarrassed others.

He was too happy to worry for long, though, about schoolteachers and their opinions. That night he sat in a third-class railway carriage, his suitcase above him on the rack, his violin case in his arms, the Munich railway station vanishing behind him.

But as he hurried south to Italy, he was doing more than merely escaping loneliness and rejoining his family; during his solitary stay in Munich, he had had time to think out certain problems, and had already made one important decision about his life.

He didn't mention this decision to his parents, when he reached Milan. He thought it better to wait—to be absolutely sure.

Then at last they were all together, in the house that his parents had rented in the city, eating a wonderful dinner, with his mother looking at him anxiously and asking him how much weight he had lost, with Maya making a great fuss over him, and with his father plainly delighted that he was home again.

Albert was pleased by his first days in Italy; spring in Milan was warm, almost tropical, after the snow and darkness of a Munich winter. He walked through the streets, looking everywhere; the people were different from the people he was used to; they seemed more cheerful, they could relax with a careless smile, a shrug; they talked so much, grew excited three times in a minute. They did not have the grim, humorless look of the crowds in downtown Munich.

"I think the people here *are* different," Maya said to him one evening, and Albert felt that he agreed with her. He already liked Milan and the Italians even more than he had thought he would. Somehow, this made it easier for him to remain true to the decision he had reached before leaving Germany.

He told his parents of his decision the next evening

at supper. "I want to give up my German citizenship," he said. "I want to do it as soon as I can."

"But why should you want to do that?" his mother asked him. Her round, good-natured face grew solemn. "It's such a strange idea. I don't know any other way to describe it."

"I knew you would think it strange," Albert said. "But don't you see?—I can't remain a German any longer. Not when I feel as I do about the government, and the Emperor. Yes, and as I feel about the people, too, for allowing themselves to have such a government."

Hermann Einstein took off his glasses and cleaned them carefully. "And what then, Albert?" he said. "After giving up your German citizenship, will you want to become an Italian or a Frenchman—or what?"

"I don't want to be the citizen of any country," Albert said. "I think, if you're a citizen, you are made to do things that are wrong. You are forced to go into the Army, you must fight in wars, and maim and kill other men—men you don't even know, men who have never done a single thing to harm you. I don't believe in wars, or in armies, or in countries that make war on other countries." His dark eyes burned passionately for a moment. "I think that war is the greatest crime that there is on earth. I would rather go to jail for the rest of my life, I would rather be torn to pieces than to be a soldier for as much as a single day."

"But couldn't you wait, Albert—must you give up your citizenship right away?" his mother said. "If you thought about it a little longer—?"

"I've already thought about it so much," he said. "And I won't change my mind, so please say you'll give me your permission. And say that you'll help me send in the right letters and papers."

"If you've really made up your mind," his father said, "then of course we'll help you. Only try to realize, Albert, what such a step could mean. It could cause you great difficulty later on. If you're a man without a country, wherever you live you will find restrictions, inconveniences—perhaps even danger. If you want *my* opinion, I think it's a very rash step to take—"

"But a step that I *must* take," Albert said. "If I'm to have any peace with myself—please—I have no other choice."

Albert's parents finally agreed to forward his papers to the German consul. They thought that he was wrong and foolish, but they saw how much it meant to him and they did not stand in his way.

In another few weeks, the necessary legal steps had been completed. At the age of sixteen, Albert was no longer a German. He was a citizen of no country. But in his own mind he had become something finer—a citizen of the world.

3

Shortly after he had renounced his German citizenship, Albert decided that he could no longer practice his religion. He thought it impossible to compromise, to accept part of anything without accepting all of it. Since he no longer believed in the literal truth of everything in the Torah, he no longer wanted to attend synagogue or to take part in religious services.

Yet he did not become an irreligious person, nor did he ever forget the ethical teachings of Judaism. Far more than he realized himself, these teachings already had become a part of his outlook, his philosophy, and they would remain so for the rest of his life.

The longer he lived the more certain he became that the Jewish tradition was a proud and an ennobling one, the Old Testament a magnificent moral creation. Many years later, he wrote these words to explain why he had always been eager to proclaim his own Jewishness: "The pursuit of knowledge for its own sake, an almost fanatical love of justice and the desire for personal independence—these are the features of the Jewish tradition which make me thank my stars that I belong to it."

The pursuit of knowledge, love of justice, the desire for personal independence—so much of Albert's life, so many of his actions, are explained by these three characteristically Jewish ideals.

With the loneliness of Munich behind him, Albert passed some of the happiest days of his life in Italy. Maya had made numerous friends, and they became Albert's friends, too. Often he and his sister were invited out for supper, and in halting Italian he tried to hold an intelligent conversation, while sampling all manner of exotic foods and listening to the strange, musical speech of his hosts.

The people he met continued to charm him. He thought that Italians were more lighthearted than the Germans, more carefree, much less willing to follow custom and routine. When an Italian felt like doing something, he did it, without asking himself whether or not it was *verboten*. Albert found his new companions warm and humane and civilized. Art and music and magnificent architecture filled their daily lives, grace and beauty surrounded them.

He spent hours by himself, standing in the Piazza del Duomo, a huge public square, gazing up at hundreds of carved figures set in niches to decorate the city's magnificent white marble cathedral. He went to the church of Santa Maria delle Grazie to see Leonardo's immortal *The Last Supper*. He visited Renaissance palaces and libraries, and thought how different the very buildings seemed from the buildings in Munich. In Milan, they were part of the scene, the landscape, a natural expression of the people and their history. In Munich, there were Renaissance palaces, too, but heavier copies of buildings seen elsewhere and built in faithful but lifeless imitation.

Completely free from compulsory studies for the first time in his life, Albert did not remain idle. He read more than ever, but only books of his own choosing. Not Greek and Latin grammars, but books which helped his own thinking, mathematical texts, and books which discussed the theories of Copernicus, Kepler, Newton, the scientific giants of the past.

Since he had so much time to himself, he decided to make further use of it, and one day he asked his parents to let him go on a walking tour. "I would only need enough money for food," he said. When they agreed that exercise in the open air might be good for his health, he started off, carrying his clothes and a few odds and ends in a knapsack.

He walked south from Milan and crossed the Apennines, stopping each night at a country inn or at a farmhouse. He lived like a vagabond, wandering where he pleased. Each day he enjoyed the sunlight, the clean air, the beauty of the countryside. Everywhere that he went, his eyes found fresh delights. Each day brought a new sense of having escaped from a dark prison into a bright and glorious world.

At Genoa he was welcomed by his cousins, the same cousins who had come to Munich to visit the Einsteins years before. When they had all been children together, these Genoa cousins had taught Albert and Maya to play a game called "Going to Sea," with old empty packing boxes for boats. Now Albert saw the real sea lying at his feet, the dazzling, matchless blue of the Mediterranean. He drew in a breath, and savored the clean, sea air, and the last dark shadows of Munich and the north seemed driven away.

Albert wandered around the city. In the Municipal Palace he saw letters written by Columbus, and more important, the violin which had once belonged to the immortal Paganini. As a moderately skilled violinist, Albert took particular interest in this violin, and thought with a moment's amusement how pleasant it would be to remove it from its glass exhibition case and test out its strings—but a look at the burly guard standing near the door persuaded him not to try it.

Soon he said good-by to his cousins and turned south again, this time following the coastline till he arrived in Pisa, the birthplace of Galileo. He visited the university where the great astronomer had studied, he walked across the same sunny courtyards and along the same narrow streets, an unknown Jewish boy, pausing for a moment to pay homage to one of his heroes.

By now his money was almost gone, but before returning to Milan, he decided to visit one more city. He left the sea behind and walked east, through the hills, till he came to Florence.

Here was the richest city in Renaissance treasures in the world. Here was the famous bridge over the Arno, the Ponte Vecchio, with its curio shops filled with gold ornaments and trinkets, here the great cathedral of Santa Maria del Fiore, with its bell tower designed by Giotto. Here were the Uffizi and the Pitti Palaces, with their vast treasure of Renaissance paintings, and public squares filled with statues of many of the world's greatest sculptors.

There wasn't enough time even to begin to see all that might be seen, but still, when he headed north again, he felt completely content. He had visited the cradle of the Renaissance, that marvelous age whose spirit had been so fearless, so eager in its search for artistic and scientific truth—an age whose spirit he could readily understand.

As he walked slowly north through the open country, back to Milan, Albert thought of all that he had seen, and then he began to think about his future. What did he plan for himself? How did he want to live?

As a free man—this much he was sure of. But

simply to be free was not enough. Free for what—to what purpose? Surely to seek after knowledge, to acquire wisdom. Though he had given up the outward forms of Judaism, he could not help obeying, instinctively, its inner principles.

He would live obscurely, then, studying the scientific problems that interested him more and more. He would take no part in the ordinary struggles of life, the pursuit of wealth or fame. He did not even understand why so many men chose to waste their lives in pursuit of them.

But his plan for the future was based on one thing: his parents having sufficient means to allow him to follow a life of study and leisure. Almost at once, on returning to Milan, he became aware of grave discussions between his mother and father about their lack of money . . . his father's face often wore a pained, worried expression.

Albert put aside his studies, and let himself be drawn into what was happening around him. His father, he learned, was in fresh difficulties. The electrical plant, far from being successful, was operating at a loss. Soon, in a few more weeks, it had to be shut down and all the equipment sold to meet mounting debts. His father had failed in business a second time.

A new round of family conferences was held. Again Albert's parents had to talk with more prosperous uncles and cousins. The Genoa branch offered a sum of money so that Hermann Einstein could start up another business, this time in the town of Pavia. Perhaps, it was said, the new location would be more favorable and would lead to success.

But Albert's position had undergone a fatal change. His dream of living quietly and following his studies, of devoting his life to examining, proving, perfecting his own ideas, this dream had vanished. His father was now a poor man, living, at least for the time being, on the generosity of relatives. Without delay, Albert would have to decide on a future career, in order to earn his own living.

Only what sort of career? his unhappy parents asked themselves. Not in business, that was out of the question. Talk of profits and losses, of sales and inventories, brought nothing but a puzzled frown to Albert's face. He could never become a successful clerk or salesman or plant manager.

His most promising asset seemed to be a brilliant mind for complicated mathematical problems. But who would pay him a single lira to write down those long, mysterious equations of his? Somehow, though, his mathematical ability would have to be used—only how?

First, his parents decided, Albert would have to return to his studies and finish high school. With a diploma, he could then go to a technical university and earn a degree in engineering. Finally, as a graduate engineer, he could work in an office or become a college teacher, and in this way he would be able to earn a livelihood for himself without going into business. There didn't seem to be any other choice.

Albert cheerfully agreed to become an engineer. He understood that he would always need money, and prepared to do his best to make himself financially independent as soon as possible.

The only thing that disturbed him was the idea of returning to high school to earn his diploma. He thought he knew of a way to enter a university without earning one. He would present the letters he had gotten from his mathematics and science teachers, testifying to the advanced work he had already done in these subjects. And he would take entrance examinations in his other subjects to prove that he could do the work and was entitled to go on to higher courses.

He refused to think of returning to Germany as his parents advised him, and at last it was settled that he would go to Switzerland, where German was spoken, and try to enter the Polytechnical School in Zurich.

Albert left Italy and took the train to Zurich, where he rented a small room. He didn't know a single person in the city, but this only meant that he would have more time to prepare for his entrance examinations. He hadn't looked at a school text for more than a year, and it seemed unlikely that a poor student could make up so much work so quickly, but he believed that with nothing to distract him it could be done.

For many dreary weeks he did nothing but schoolwork. Finally the day came for the examinations. Afterward, he was too tired to know whether he had done well or not. Hopefully, he awaited a summons to the office of Dr. Herzog, Director of the Polytechnical School.

After several days, he was called to the Director's office. "You have failed to qualify," Dr. Herzog said.

The Director saw the light die in Albert's eyes. He was touched by the way the young man's shoulders sagged, and by his slow footsteps as he dragged himself away to the door.

"Wait, come back," the Director said. He made Albert take a chair, and listened to his story. Then he told Albert that his tests in mathematics and physics had been extremely good, even brilliant. His other tests had been poor. He had failed in languages, botany, and zoology.

The Director suggested a plan. If Albert were willing to go to a Swiss high school for a few months, he could easily make up the subjects he had failed, and would receive his diploma. Then he could enter the Polytechnical School without further delay, to begin studying for an engineering degree.

Albert thanked him, and returned to his dark, empty room.

To begin all over again—to go back to another "gymnasium," to the brutality, the stupidity, the boredom, the endless memorizing of unimportant facts and dates and names. To be a slave again—everything in his soul rebelled against such a decision.

Yet a free man, he knew, must meet his responsibilities. And Albert's first responsibility was to enter college and make himself financially independent. If it meant returning to slavery for a time, then he must return to slavery.

A few days later, he enrolled in the "gymnasium" at a place called Aarau, a country town not far from Zurich. He was seventeen, he had not finished high school, he had not passed his examinations—he was, he told himself, an utter failure.

4

In Aarau, Albert's mood of despair quickly disappeared. He discovered to his surprise that going to high school in Switzerland was quite different from going to high school in Germany.

Swiss students were encouraged to think for themselves. They were allowed to ask questions when they did not understand something. Their classrooms were not run like an army camp, and so, when they were called on by a teacher, they were not expected to leap to their feet and stand as stiff as soldiers before answering him, but to remain in their seats and to speak in a perfectly natural way.

The Swiss teachers were friendly and understanding. After a class was over, they were ready to help a student if he wished to seek advice about his work, or if he had any further questions to ask about the lecture.

The head of the school in Aarau was a kindhearted and generous man named Professor Winteler. One day the professor met Albert on the stairs and said to him, "You must come to my house for dinner one night this week, Albert. I want you to meet my family. If I say so myself, I have a fair-sized brood. Seven children. A son about your own age. Do come—I think you will enjoy it."

Albert accepted the invitation, and found from the start that he liked the Wintelers as much as they liked him. There was a spare room in their home, and Albert was soon asked if he would care to move in with the family, for as long as he stayed in Aarau? He said that he very much would, and before the end of the week he was installed there as a regular member of the household.

The Wintelers lived in much the same way as Albert's own family had lived in Munich. The atmosphere in the professor's house was friendly and informal, and Albert never felt any of his usual shyness while he was there.

Several of the professor's children played musical instruments, and with Albert joining them on his violin, they often held chamber music concerts in the family living room.

When the weather was fine, Albert and the Wintelers took long walks together through the mountains and the pine forests, which looked so much like the mountains and forests that Albert remembered from his childhood in Bavaria. When spring came, they began to go for picnics on the nearby lakes, exactly as Albert and his family had done when they had lived in Munich.

Professor Winteler tutored Albert in a number of his subjects, especially in foreign languages, and with the professor's help, Albert passed his examinations at the end of the school year. He had finally earned his high school diploma. Now, he was ready to enter the Polytechnical School in Zurich, to study for his graduate degree.

On the summer day when Albert took the train from Aarau to go to Italy for a few weeks, the entire Winteler family came down to the railroad station to see him off. Albert felt very sad at parting from these kindly people who had treated him as if he had been their own son.

The Wintelers were just as sad to see Albert leave. They made him promise that he would keep in touch with them, and this he always did faithfully. In fact, a few years later, he introduced one of the professor's sons to Maya, and before long they were married, so that Albert and the Wintelers eventually became closer than ever.

In the fall, Albert began his college studies in Zurich. His father was still having great financial trouble, though, and could give him no money to live on. Fortunately, a rich uncle agreed to send Albert one hundred Swiss francs each month for four years, until he had completed his work at the Polytechnical School.

One hundred Swiss francs was worth about twenty American dollars. Not a large sum, but Albert learned to do without luxuries and even without some of the things that are usually thought to be necessities.

He had no new clothes. He often cooked his own meals at home to save money, and when he did eat out, it was only in the cheapest restaurants. He never entertained or spent the evening at a party, and his only extravagance was a ticket, high up in the balcony, on the rare occasions when he went to a local concert.

His room was small and dingy, in the old part of the city, with a dusty window overlooking a dark, winding street. It was far removed from the modern part of Zurich, which was smart and clean and filled with sunlight —and where prices for rent and heat were much higher.

To add to his small allowance, he tutored some of the slower students at school in their mathematics courses, but this gained him little extra money, because most of them were as poor as Albert was himself. And when a student told him that he could not afford to pay him anything at all, Albert said, "All right, it makes no difference, I'll help you for nothing then."

The more time that Albert spent in Switzerland, the more he came to admire the country and its people. Switzerland, he learned, was among the most democratic nations in Europe. It had been a republic since the end of the thirteenth century, longer than any other country in the world. The Swiss were intensely proud of their personal and political freedom. And they were not in the least a warlike people. They did arm and train for the defense of their country, but they had no ambition to grow strong and rich at the expense of their neighbors. The Swiss were as peace-loving as Albert himself, and he felt that if he could have chosen the place of his birth, it might very well have been this democratic republic in the heart of Europe.

He decided that after he had finished his graduate studies at the Polytechnical School, he would like to become a teacher in a Swiss high school or university, but there was one difficulty to this plan. In order to teach in Switzerland, he would first have to become a Swiss citizen.

Albert did not really mind this. He was older, a little bit wiser now. He knew that a man was better off, had more freedom to move about, if he was a citizen of *some* country. And Switzerland certainly suited Albert the best.

To pay for his citizenship papers, he had to begin saving money at once, so that he didn't even have one hundred francs a month to live on. He had to keep out no less than twenty, and this he managed to do by buying cheaper food—and sometimes by buying less of it.

As poor as he was, Albert found that in one way he was happier than he had ever been before. At the Polytechnical School, for the first time in his life, he was able to spend a few hours each day with companions who were interested in the same subjects that he was interested in. With these companions he was able to discuss his thoughts, and to be understood. He was also able to hear of new ideas and to profit from them.

At the Polytechnical School, he made three good friends, Marcel Grossmann, a young Swiss student, Friederich Adler, an Austrian, and Mileva Maritsch, a girl student from Hungary.

Once, Marcel Grossmann helped Albert out when he was in serious difficulty at school. Shortly before an important examination, they met after classes, and as a special treat, had supper together at a cheap restaurant.

But Albert said he didn't feel like eating. He confessed that he was worried. He told his friend that he had not been doing the work for one of their courses. He had been too absorbed in his own thoughts, in developing his own ideas. In fact, he had not been to any of the lectures for the course in months—they had seemed like such a waste of time.

Marcel admired Albert's abilities tremendously. He knew that his friend could pass any scientific course if only he would take some trouble and make the effort to do so. And he said to Albert, "Don't worry, I can fix things for you. Let's eat our supper first and enjoy ourselves. Then we'll go back to my place and I'll show you something that should suprise you."

Later, they returned to Marcel's room, where he took out a large leather-bound notebook and opened it. "Here you are," he said to Albert. "Just study these before the exam and you'll get through with an excellent mark."

Albert looked at the notebook. His friend had kept a complete record of the lectures, with notes that filled in everything to the last detail. In a few hours, Albert had read and understood the work that had occupied the rest of the class for months. He took the examination and passed it easily, and afterwards he thanked Marcel again for the use of his notebook.

Marcel was delighted. He believed that Albert was an exceptionally gifted student, and he was perfectly willing to help him avoid the time-wasting routine of some of the lecture courses which he knew that Albert deeply resented. Marcel was one of the first men in the world to sense, though it could only have been in a vague way, the importance of the work that Albert had already begun to undertake on his own.

Friederich Adler was another of Albert's friends at the Polytechnical School. Friederich's father was the leader of the Socialist Party in Austria, and he had sent Friederich to Zurich to keep him out of political activities—to keep him out of trouble, really.

Like Albert, Friederich was a pacifist; through their talks, Albert came to see that there were people in every country in Europe who believed that war was evil, that it could even be prevented, if there were an international organization capable of settling arguments between nations. Albert's talks with Friederich made him feel sure that if intelligent, peace-loving people would only band together, there was a chance to make the world over, to turn it into a better place for men to live.

During his four years at the Polytechnical School, Albert's scientific ideas were growing clearer. He finally saw what he wanted to do in the future—in his spare time—when he wasn't teaching. Theoretical physics would be his field of study. He hoped, and believed it possible, that all of the physical properties of the universe could eventually be explained by a few brief mathematical equations. It might take years to formulate these equations, and equally as long to find out if they were true or not, but Albert felt sure of one thing—in order to do this work he would not need to study any more mathematics.

In time, he learned that he had made a mistake. Often, in later years, he had to have the assistance of mathematicians, to help test his theories, because his own mathematical studies had stopped short and his knowledge of the field was too limited to let him proceed without help.

But before he gave up studying mathematics, he met Mileva Maritsch in one of his classes. She was pretty, dark-haired, quiet, with a brilliant mind and a rather moody and unstable disposition. She had lived in Hungary, but she was Serbian. The Serbs were one of several minority races that lived under the foreign rule of the Austro-Hungarian Empire.

Albert, who often felt uneasy with strangers, especially with young women—they generally acted in ways that he found quite mysterious—felt no uneasiness with Mileva. She understood the work that interested him, and she was able to listen with intelligence while he spoke of the latest ideas that he was developing. His need for affection, for love, was suddenly answered. They became constant companions, and announced that they would be married as soon as Albert had graduated and had found a job.

In the spring of 1900, Albert received his graduate degree in engineering from the Polytechnical School. His professors congratulated him warmly, said that he was a brilliant student, and made many polite remarks about his bright future as a teacher and a theoretical physicist.

It seemed that finally all of Albert's troubles were over. But strangely enough, the most cruel and painful months in his life were about to begin.

5

Usually, when a high-ranking student like Albert had finished his course of study at the Polytechnical School and had announced his intention of becoming a teacher, it was the custom for one of his professors to hire him as an assistant. But in Albert's case, none of the professors seemed to remember the custom.

Weeks passed, and Albert still did not have a job. So, one after another, he began to visit his professors. He went to their offices, or their laboratories, and talked with them.

They were very polite. They were very friendly. They were sure, of course, that he would find something suitable quite soon—by the way, had he gone to see professor so-and-so yet? Perhaps *he* might be able to help—but the one thing they did not say was, "Mr. Einstein, will you be *my* assistant?"

Slowly Albert came to realize that his professors were

not going to help him. Amazed and bewildered, he returned to his room, and tried to imagine what had happened.

Why had they turned against him? What could the reason be?

Perhaps they were afraid to hire him. Perhaps they didn't want an assistant whose scientific ideas they disapproved of—or, Albert thought with a wry smile, whose ideas they couldn't even be sure they understood. An assistant who might hold them up to embarrassment or ridicule—what a tiresome sort of assistant *that* would be! Well, if they were afraid of him, Albert felt that he could forgive them. Fear was an understandable human weakness—yes, he was quite sure he could forgive them for that.

Then, Albert thought of another reason why they might have been unwilling to hire him. He had been a Swiss citizen for only a few months. Some of his professors were very conservative in their political thinking. They were as much afraid of a "new" citizen as they were of a new scientific idea. They believed that only native-born Swiss should be hired to teach in Swiss technical schools and universities. Albert found it much more difficult to forgive his professors for their foolishly "patriotic" point of view.

Finally, as some of Albert's friends began to insist, there was still a third possibility. Albert was a Jew. Perhaps his professors might have overlooked his scientific ideas, they might even have overlooked his recent citizenship—but wasn't his being Jewish one fault too many—the proverbial straw that broke the camel's back?

Albert, as he began to see that this was probably the real explanation, found that he could no longer forgive his professors for the way they had acted. To think ill of a man because he belonged to a particular race or religion—this was too much to forgive. As men of science, their conduct was especially shameful. For science itself was the one field of knowledge most completely without barriers—a man was a scientist, no matter what his race or religion or his native language. The conduct of his professors was absurd—and worse than absurd—it was evil.

If he had ever been inclined to suppose that anti-Semitism was exclusively a religious problem, Albert could never do so again. He might well have thought, that summer in Zurich, when he needed a job so badly and when his being a Jew was used to prevent him from finding one, "Yes, if a man is born a Jew, he remains a Jew for the rest of his life. He need not hold conventional religious opinions, he need not worship in a synagogue—he will still be treated as a Jew, and made an object of hatred and bigotry because of his birth."

For the first time, Albert began to study closely the evils of anti-Semitism. His experience in Zurich that summer made him curious about the conditions under which Jews were forced to live in different European countries, and it aroused him to a new interest in their welfare. For if a Jew could suffer from anti-Semitism in Switzerland—the most liberal and democratic country in Europe—what could they not suffer in countries like Poland and Germany and Russia, where there was little liberal thought and no democracy at all?

But at the moment, he was too distracted by his own troubles to have much time to think of the problems of others. Each day his position was becoming more serious. He was no longer receiving one hundred francs a month from his rich uncle. His uncle had been willing to help Albert obtain a college degree, but he certainly had no intention of doing any more for him. The month Albert graduated, the money stopped arriving at the post office.

Albert's small savings were almost completely used up. He tried for any kind of teaching position. He wrote to other Swiss colleges and universities, sending letters from his own professors saying that he was a brilliant scholar—but he was not offered work. He applied at high schools and was turned down. He read newspaper advertisements and answered any that called for a science or a mathematics teacher—all without success.

He was nearly in despair. His clothes had grown shabby, and this did not help when he had to apply for a job in person. He began to skip meals, and sometimes did not eat for a couple of days at a time, in order to conserve his last few francs.

Then, finally, he had some luck. He was accepted for a temporary job as a substitute teacher at a vocational high school. The high school was located in the nearby industrial village of Winterthur.

His first day in class, the students thought they would have some fun with the substitute teacher. He looked too young to be worth much anyway. There was hidden laughter as he introduced himself and turned to the blackboard. But soon the students were listening in spite of themselves. Albert talked easily, and presented the subject clearly, in words that all of the students could understand. They forgot his youth, his shy manner. They listened, as they never had before.

For two months, Albert taught them, and for two months he and his students got along well together. Then the regular teacher returned to the school, and Albert was out of a job again.

His position soon grew worse than ever. He was almost in rags, his shirts frayed at the collar and cuffs, the soles of his shoes worn thin, his trousers shiny in the seat. He ate only one meal a day, and the cheap and unwholesome food that he did eat affected his stomach. He was sick for several weeks, and afterward he was never entirely free from a weak digestion and stomach trouble.

Then, through a newspaper advertisement, he learned of a teaching job in a town called Schaffhausen, where a "gymnasium" teacher ran a special private school on the side. Albert went there and was hired to tutor two backward students.

For a while he enjoyed his work. He found that teaching young children was a pleasant task—their minds were so much more free of prejudice, so much more ready to accept new ideas than the minds of most adults. Children weren't afraid to admit that they didn't know something, they were willing to ask why? as Albert was so often forced to ask when he was working on his own problems.

In Schaffhausen, he tried to develop teaching methods that were better than those he had known himself as a small boy in Munich. He tried to interest his pupils, to arouse their curiosity. But he soon learned that whatever he did to encourage his pupils was just so much wasted effort.

The other teachers were completely old-fashioned. They wanted the students to memorize names and dates, to repeat in their examinations what they had read in their schoolbooks, to think exactly as they were told to think. That's what students had always done, and that's what they would continue to do in Schaffhausen.

When Albert spoke to the head of the school, and asked for special permission to teach his two pupils in all their subjects so that the other teachers couldn't interfere, the head of the school saw in the request a criticism of his own teaching methods—and fired Albert from the school that afternoon.

Albert's fortunes were now at their lowest ebb. Not only had he and Mileva been forced to postpone their marriage, it seemed likely that they would never be able to get married at all. He was penniless. The last of his clothes were worn out. He was virtually starving.

Then, Albert's former college classmate, Marcel Grossmann, proved what a true friend he really was. He had heard of Albert's plight, and one day he hurried to Albert's room in Zurich. He had an idea. His father knew a man named Haller, the Director of the patent office in Berne.

"You must go there at once," Marcel said. "They have an opening for a patent examiner. No—don't tell me—I realize you don't know anything about patents and inventions, but I'm sure you can do the work if they'll only hire you. Come on, come on, this may be exactly the chance you've been looking for."

Marcel half-dragged Albert to the railroad station, where he bought Albert's ticket as well as his own. Then the two friends rode to Berne, where Marcel introduced Albert to Mr. Haller.

Mr. Haller took Albert into his office and talked with him for several hours. He questioned Albert, to see

what his technical training had been, and to find out
how much he had learned at the Polytechnical School.
"But I don't know anything about inventions," Albert said at one point, compelled to be honest and to
avoid telling lies, despite his desperate need for the
job. "I mustn't deceive you, Mr. Haller. I mustn't pre-
tend that I've had experience in this sort of work, when
I haven't."

Mr. Haller said that he understood this. He was not
particularly interested in Albert's previous experience. "What I want," he said, "is a young man with a
mathematical turn of mind, who can think logically.
He will have to study all of the dozens of drawings and
blueprints that come here every day. Some of these
come from cranks, and some from real inventors. He
will have to separate them, and then he will have to
decide if a patent can be awarded for the real inventions.
As I've said before, he must be a young man who can
think logically, and I see that you can do that."

He pointed to a copy of Albert's college record.
"Anyone who can complete such a course of study with
these excellent marks can certainly understand the
work here. The job is yours, Mr. Einstein—if you want
it."

"Thank you, thank you very much," Albert said.
"Of course, I do want it, Mr. Haller. When shall I report
to you?"

Within a few days, Albert had moved his few possessions to Berne and was working at his desk in the Swiss patent office. The year was 1902. And as unlikely as it seems, it was in this office that a revolution in scientific thought took place that would eventually change the entire course of human history.

6

After a few weeks in Berne, Albert began to realize how fortunate he was to have obtained a job in the Swiss patent office. The work was easy for him, and he took pleasure in doing it.

Each morning he opened the mail and spread out the plans for new inventions on his desk. He studied the plans, and then decided which inventions deserved a patent and which did not. For Albert, this work was as enjoyable as solving a series of puzzles. He had as much fun out of his daily "inventions" as another man would have had playing a game of chess or a rubber of bridge.

Before long he found that he could easily finish his work in three or four hours each day, and this gave him the chance to do whatever he pleased in the afternoons. He was careful not to mention the fact to Mr. Haller or to his fellow workers, but soon he started to bring his own papers to the office. He kept them hidden in a drawer of his desk. Whenever he had finished with the day's inventions, he took these papers out and thought about the ideas and problems that really interested him.

A regular job meant regular meals, a small but pleasant room to live in, and enough money to support a family. In 1903, after less than a year in Berne, he married Mileva Maritsch, and the next year they had a son, the first of their two boys.

Albert was perfectly content with his new life. He had a growing family, an interesting job, and enough time to do his own work. And his own work was beginning to please him. Some of his ideas were almost finished, they were almost ready to be shown to the world. He spent more and more time on them, not only at the office but in the evenings at home, after supper. He toiled without letup, tirelessly, week after week, month after month.

Finally, one afternoon in 1905, when he was only twenty-six years old, he went to the office of the editor of a little Swiss scientific magazine called *Annalen der Physik*, "*The Yearbook of Physics*," and left a number of pages of his work on the editor's desk.

Each year since 1901, Albert had published a single article in the *Yearbook*. None of the articles had attracted much notice. This time, he left five articles with the editor.

When he came out of the office and reached the

street, he felt suddenly faint. He arrived home, pale and trembling, and Mileva had to help him to bed.

She wanted to send for the doctor, but he told her not to. "I'm tired, that's all," he said. "Soon, I will be all right again."

Two weeks went by before he was strong enough to return to his regular job at the patent office. It was as though all of his strength had been used up, completing his work.

The first two articles that Albert had left on the editor's desk were not outstanding. They talked about ideas that were already familiar to other scientists. They were well-written, but not original or surprising.

The third, fourth, and fifth articles were a different matter.

Many years later, Albert was awarded a Nobel Prize, the most important prize in the world that a scientist can win, and he was awarded it for the third article in the *Yearbook*. This article talked about something that scientists call "the photoelectrical effect." Modern television was made possible by the work that Albert did on this subject.

Albert never won a Nobel Prize for the fourth article, but he won everlasting fame because of it. In later years, when scientists came to understand what he had written, they said that this fourth article contained one of the most important scientific theories ever developed in the history of mankind—the Special Theory of Relativity.

There is no way to explain all of the Special Theory of Relativity without using words and ideas that only highly trained scientists and mathematicians can understand. But it is possible to describe in a simple way a few of the subjects that the theory deals with.

The nature of "light" is one of these subjects. Everything in the universe, except light, Albert said, appears to travel at different speeds under different circumstances.

For instance, to an observer, seated far away from some railroad tracks, a passing train will appear to be moving slowly—to an observer near the tracks, the same train will appear to be moving quickly—while to a passenger inside the train, if he looks down at the floor, the train will not appear to be moving at all.

Only light, in empty space, appears to travel at the same speed to all observers. This is true, whether the observer himself is traveling toward the source of light or away from it.

This is a strange paradox, and Albert explained it by suggesting the revolutionary idea that objects will appear to change their size and shape as their speed changes, and he provided a mathematical formula to predict what the change would be.

The fourth of Albert's articles talked, in part, of the

universe and of the stars, many of which are millions of times larger than our own sun. Albert's fifth and last article talked about one of the smallest things in the universe—the atom.

An atom is too small for us to see, even under the most powerful microscope. But there are billions and trillions of atoms everywhere: in the clothes we wear, the water we drink, the pencils we write with, the paper we write on. Even our own bodies are made up of different kinds of atoms.

Albert said something about the atom that nobody had ever said before. And because he was a scientist, he said it in the language that scientists often use—he said it in the form of an equation. It is perhaps the most famous equation in history:

$$E = MC^2$$

In this equation, Albert said, E stands for "Energy" —which is a measure of a quantity of work—M stands for "Mass"—which is very similar to weight—and C^2 stands for the speed of light (186,000 miles per second) multiplied by itself (186,000 × 186,000).

What this equation really meant was this: that in every atom there was a tremendous force, a tremendous amount of energy, waiting to be released, and that one day man might convert atoms into energy and use this energy to change the world.

A few years later, a professor in Vienna studied Albert's equation and said this about it: "It takes one's breath away to think what might happen in a town, if the energy of a single brick were to be set free, say in the form of an explosion. . . . This, however, will never happen. . . ."

In time, of course, it did happen. We learned to start and control an atomic explosion. We learned to build the first atomic bomb. And the age we live in takes its name from these events. We say now that we are living in the Atomic Age—the age that Albert's famous equation first made possible.

After Albert had recovered some of his strength, he returned to the patent office and began to live and work exactly as he had before. He knew that his articles would soon be published in the *Yearbook*, and he hoped that they would be read and understood by at least a few of his fellow scientists. That was all that he hoped for.

He didn't think that the articles would change his life. He didn't want his life changed. He wanted to go on living in Berne, earning enough money for his family, pursuing his own thoughts, as he had been doing so peacefully for the past four years.

It was still 1905. Volume 17 of the *Yearbook* had just come off the printing press. Its pages were tied between covers, its few copies were sealed in envelopes, and finally they were mailed to readers in every country in Europe. The Theory of Relativity and the great equation E=MC² were given to the world for the first time. And afterward—nothing happened. Absolutely nothing.

No one came rushing to Berne to find Albert, to seize his hand, to say, "Mr. Einstein, the world is in your debt for what you have done!"

There were no newspaper headlines, no public meetings—and Albert, of course, did not expect them. He did expect, though, that his last three articles would have created *some* interest . . . but as far as he could tell, not one scientist in the world had taken the least notice of what he had written.

Month after month went by, and there was only silence. Apparently, his ideas were to be ignored.

If Albert felt any disappointment, he didn't show it. Perhaps he was puzzled when he failed to receive even a single letter about his work, but he knew that there are many things in the world that are puzzling, and so he shrugged, and tried to think no more about it.

What actually had been happening all these months was somewhat different from what Albert had imagined. His theory of relativity, far from being ignored, was simply not understood.

Most scientists who read it refused to believe that it could be true. Among his former teachers, there were some who said, "I knew it—I said when this Einstein was here at the Polytechnical School—'he's very unstable. . . .' Really, if what he says in this theory of his were true, why, it would overturn everything that people have believed for the last three hundred years. So it can't be true . . . I think he's talking a lot of nonsense, don't you agree?"

A few important scientists in Switzerland did not agree. The theory of relativity might be true or untrue—they couldn't be sure—but in either case, it was the work of a brilliant man. "Who *is* this Albert Einstein?" they began to ask.

"Yes—and where does he lecture? At which of our Swiss universities is he a professor?"

And when the answer began to come back, that Albert Einstein was really only an examiner in the Federal Patent Office in Berne, their astonishment was immense.

"Impossible! I simply do not believe it!"

"A man with his mind! In the patent office!"

"It's fantastic! An examiner in Berne!"

Astonishment came first, and then these important Swiss scientists began to feel a terrible sense of uneasiness and embarrassment.

How was it that he had even thought of working at the patent office? How was it that he did not have a professorship somewhere in Switzerland, a regular position as a teacher and lecturer? Why had no one realized that here was a man with a truly brilliant mind—why had no one looked out for him, done something to see that he could continue his work in peace?

Finally, after many months, one or two letters, asking some of these questions, began to arrive at Albert's apartment.

He answered the letters very politely, and did not say unpleasant things about his former teachers at the Polytechnical School. He rarely bore grudges, and he had long since forgiven his teachers for the shabby way they had treated him.

Now he could even smile when he thought of the terrible poverty he had known a few years before. How desperately he had needed a teaching job then. But, he told the Swiss scientists, when he answered their letters, he certainly didn't need a teaching job now. He wasn't even sure that he would accept one if somebody decided to offer it to him.

No—he thanked them—but he was really quite happy here in Berne. He preferred to remain exactly where he was, doing exactly what he wanted to do.

The world, though, had begun to suspect the importance of Albert's ideas. Only a small part of the world, a little group of embarrassed Swiss scientists, but their suspicion would soon draw him away from the patent office, and from the most peaceful and quiet days he was to know for the rest of his life.

7

In 1906 an important man interested himself in Albert's affairs. He was Professor Kleiner, the leading member of the physics department at the university in Zurich. Professor Kleiner did not really understand Albert's ideas, but he was sure that Albert was a brilliant scientist, and if he possibly could, he wanted to bring him into the physics department at the university.

Despite his own wish to remain at the patent office, Albert recognized that a professorship at a university would be very valuable to him. It would give him a chance to meet many scientists who were interested in the same problems that he was interested in, it would permit him to benefit from an exchange of ideas, and it would eventually mean that he would be able to earn more money to support his wife and two small children.

So Albert made up his mind that he would have to become a professor. But, as so often happened, there was an unforeseen difficulty.

Albert learned of this difficulty when Professor Kleiner came to Berne to visit him. No one, it seemed, could be appointed a professor at a Swiss university, without first becoming a *privatdozent*—that is, a sort of "junior" professor who gave lectures for a year or two, in order to prove his ability to teach. His only pay was a small fee, collected from the students who came to his lectures.

"But this will never do," Albert told the professor. "I have a wife and family to support. Now, you say to me, 'Give up your job here in Berne, and move to Zurich, and work as a *privatdozent* for a year or two at no salary at all, and then we will make you a professor.' Yes—but in the meantime, what will I do to feed and clothe my family? Where will the money come from?"

Professor Kleiner said to Albert, "I don't know where it will come from, Mr. Einstein, but I *do* know that you *must* serve as a *privatdozent*—there is no way to avoid it. Before I can get you a professorship at our university, you must first give a series of lectures, so as to qualify under the rules and regulations."

Even though they were discussing a serious matter, Albert was very much tempted to smile. *More* rules and regulations—really, it seemed that university professors were no different from high school teachers. They too believed that rules and regulations were the most important things in the world.

Finally Albert shook his head. "Then I can't do what

you suggest," he said. "If I were to give up my job here in Berne, I would soon be penniless. My family would starve. So, I'm afraid that I cannot become a professor after all."

Professor Kleiner understood Albert's problem, and sympathized with his need for money. He was also very determined to have Albert become a member of his department, and he suggested this compromise: if it could be arranged, would Albert be willing to keep his present job at the patent office, and deliver a series of lectures in his spare time at the university in Berne—instead of at the university in Zurich?

"Then," the professor said, "after you've given the proper number of lectures to qualify, I will do my utmost to bring you to Zurich as a professor with a regular salary."

"Yes, that I will be willing to do," Albert said. And so he remained in Berne, working as a patent examiner, and to satisfy the "rules and regulations," he began to give a series of lectures at the nearby university.

These lectures very nearly ruined Albert's chance of becoming a professor. He really didn't want to give any lectures. His mind was bursting with fresh ideas about the theory of relativity, and he felt that he had to spend at least a part of each day developing them. He had no time to spare, preparing a series of lectures that the average college student could understand.

So he didn't prepare them. Instead, he came to the

class and talked about relativity, and his students, after one or two hours of this, decided that they couldn't make heads or tails out of Mr. Einstein's course, and went to somebody else's lectures.

One day, Professor Kleiner paid a surprise visit to Berne, to see how successful Albert was as a lecturer. When he came into the lecture hall, he was hardly pleased by what he saw.

It was a large room, and very nearly empty. Only two seats were filled. Two students—and it turned out that they were Albert's friends.

While the professor watched, Albert stood at the blackboard, describing his complicated thoughts, pausing to jot down an equation, then pausing even longer, to consider what he was going to say next. Sometimes there were several minutes of silence, while Albert decided what point he wanted to explain.

This, Professor Kleiner thought, is not the correct way to give a lecture. And he said so to Albert when the hour was over. He told Albert that the subject matter was much too difficult. No wonder all his students had been frightened away. Furthermore, the lecture itself was poorly planned, badly organized. It was, the professor assured him, a most unsatisfactory performance.

Albert was neither hurt nor angered by this criticism. He felt he must speak the truth, and he said to Professor Kleiner, in a calm, almost gentle voice, "Well, I didn't *ask* to be appointed a professor at the university—did I?" And there was very little that Professor Kleiner could say in reply.

Between 1906 and 1908 Albert continued to lecture to empty classrooms in Berne, and to live there in obscurity. The people of the city had no idea that he was anything except an unimportant civil servant who walked about with a pipe in his mouth and a kindly and rather absent expression on his face.

But among scientists and mathematicians, word of his theory had begun to spread. In Prague, Warsaw, Berlin, they turned to the *Yearbook of Physics* and read his articles. A few scientists said he was a madman, and set to work to prove that the theory of relativity was a hoax.

Most of his readers, though, were deeply impressed. *If* what Einstein says is true, they told one another, then he is a most remarkable man—probably the most remarkable man of our generation—and perhaps of the last three or four hundred years.

Yes—*if* what he says is true. But we must have proof, and it may be years before we have it. Let us think twice before we make too much of Einstein—it's better to be on the safe side, when you can't be sure.

As the months passed, Albert began to receive invitations to deliver lectures to scientific societies throughout Europe, invitations that would continue to come to him for the rest of his life. And though traveling meant an extra expense that he could not easily afford, he willingly went wherever he was invited, because he welcomed the chance to explain his ideas to other scientists, and to learn as much as he could from them.

One of the men he met on a lecture trip in 1908 was the Dutch scientist Hendrik Lorenz, who did a great deal to bring Albert's name before the scientific world. A warm friendship sprang up between them, the first and one of the deepest that Albert formed with a number of scientists and famous men.

In the meantime, in Zurich, Professor Kleiner continued to do all that he could to have Albert appointed to a professorship at the university there. At last, there was an opening. The professor saw his chance, and put forward Albert's name. Almost at once, a new difficulty arose.

Another professor suggested someone else for the position. By a strange coincidence, the young man suggested was one of Albert's former college friends, Friederich Adler.

For a time, it looked as if Friederich would receive the professorship instead of Albert. But when Friederich heard of the situation, he immediately wrote to the university and said, "If you can get a man like Einstein . . . it would be absurd to appoint me. . . . My ability as a physicist does not bear even the slightest comparison to Einstein's."

It was a remarkable gesture of integrity, and it decided the issue. Soon after, Albert was appointed to the professorship. When he discovered what Friederich had written, he was deeply touched. He knew that his friend had acted with a generosity that few other men would have been able to match.

In 1909 Albert and Mileva moved back to Zurich, where they remained for a year. They found a number of friends from their college days who were still in the city. At night, they often had guests for supper, and sometimes, after the table was cleared, Albert took out his violin and played Mozart sonatas for their entertainment.

During the day, when he was free from work, he loved to take his two small sons for a walk, and his neighbors grew used to the sight of the young professor as he strolled along the street, proudly pushing a baby carriage ahead of him.

Albert was especially happy in his work. Now that he didn't have to spend the day at the patent office, he enjoyed giving lectures, and he prepared them carefully. He felt that he had time to spare, and he spent it helping his students. "Come to see me whenever you wish," he told them. "You will not disturb me—I can stop my thoughts when you come and start them again when you leave. Bring me your problems, I will enjoy helping you solve them."

Strangely enough, now that he was finally a professor, Albert was worse off financially than he had been as a patent examiner. In Berne, he had been able to live the simplest sort of life. But in Zurich, as a member of the university faculty, he was expected to wear more expensive clothes, to invite other professors and their wives out to dinner, to go to the theater—in short, to keep up appearances. His professorship was one of the lowest grade and did not pay a large salary. He and Mileva had to take students into their apartment and charge them rent in order to make ends meet at the end of the month.

And so, when Albert was asked to join the faculty of the German University at Prague, as a full professor and at a much higher salary, he was strongly tempted to accept the offer and move again.

The trouble was, he knew how much Mileva wanted to remain in Zurich. It was the one place in the world, she said, where she felt at peace. Prague was in the Austro-Hungarian Empire, and Mileva's people, the Serbians, were a part of that empire, an unfortunate minority to whom the Austrians refused independence and whom they treated very badly. "I shall never be happy in Prague," Mileva said, but she finally agreed to go there if it was necessary.

She and Albert had already begun to find their marriage less satisfactory than it had been before. In Prague, Albert thought, if she is very unhappy, what will happen to us? Will we drift even farther apart?

While he was trying to decide whether or not to accept the new professorship, a problem arose which showed how much Albert had changed in certain of his beliefs and attitudes.

Before his appointment at Prague could be approved, he had to fill out various official forms and papers. On one form, he was asked to state his religion. Many of his friends cautioned him to avoid saying that he was Jewish. Some of the university professors at Prague were known to be anti-Semitic. It might keep him from receiving the appointment.

But once he made up his mind to go to Prague, Albert did not hesitate. The boy of sixteen who had thought he could turn his back on Judaism had grown into a much wiser man of thirty-one. Though he didn't attend services, he knew that he had remained a Jew. He believed in God, the designer of the universe, the creator of all that was beautiful, all that was harmonious. He knew that his personal philosophy had been greatly influenced by his early religious instruction. The aims of his life were Jewish aims: to search for truth, God's truth, to try to attain an understanding of the divine plan for all creation.

And Albert wrote, in his clear hand, "Religion—Jewish," and mailed the forms to the German University in Prague without a moment's doubt or hesitation.

8

A few weeks after he had sent his papers to the German University in Prague, Albert received word that his appointment was approved. He was a full professor at last, with a salary that would meet the needs of his wife and children.

Early in the fall, he and Mileva and their two sons left Switzerland. They took a train to the east and traveled through the Austrian province of Bohemia, until finally they reached Prague, the capital. Here they rented a large, pleasant apartment. They had many comforts that they had never previously been able to afford. Yet as time began to pass, Albert realized with sorrow that he and Mileva had drifted so far apart that their marriage itself was in danger of failing.

They no longer found the same contentment in one another's company that they had found during their first years together in Switzerland. They tried to understand what was wrong, but during the months that they were in Prague, their unhappiness grew stronger. Slowly they learned the truth about themselves. They simply were not suited to each other; they could not make their home life a happy one.

Albert sought to relieve his sadness by throwing himself into his work, and by observing, in his spare time, the life of the people in this part of the Austrian Empire.

Bohemia was a confusing country, quite unlike any other that he had seen. At times he was perplexed, at times even amused by the way it was run, but more often he was made angry by the many political and social injustices which existed under the rule of the Austrian Emperor.

Prague was a hopelessly divided city. Most of its citizens were Czechoslovakian, but the city was ruled by a small Austrian minority, a German-speaking people, whose attitudes and feelings were predominantly German, too.

There was great bitterness and distrust between the Austrians and the Czechs. The Austrians thought the Czechs were an inferior race, and treated them with contempt. The Czechs, who longed for political independence, thought the Austrians were arrogant and cruel and overbearing, and treated them with a sullen hatred that often threatened to break out in open revolt.

Feelings had become so strong that, a number of years before, the university itself had been divided into two separate universities. In one, only German was spoken, in the other, only Czechoslovakian. Each university had its own professors, and the two groups rarely mixed.

Albert detested this racial antagonism. He thought that the Austrians were primarily to blame for the unrest in Prague and Bohemia. They ruled the country and they should have ruled it wisely. They should have shown tolerance for the Czechs, and for the other Slavic peoples who lived within the borders of their empire. Instead, they tried to crush the Czechs, tried to keep them from having any measure of real independence, and they did this, they said, because the Czechs were so "backward" and "primitive" that they weren't capable of governing themselves.

Here, Albert began to realize, were evil seeds for the future. An arrogant ruling class, a lack of political freedom, an intense hatred between races—the city was being poisoned by these things, as much of Europe itself was being poisoned.

Nineteen eleven was a year of growing unrest throughout the world. In Europe, many countries were increasing the size of their armies. Many countries were claiming land that belonged to their neighbors. Many races, like the Czechs and the Slovenes, were demanding their independence. And throughout the world, men began to fear that there might be no way to prevent the outbreak of a general war.

In fact, that year, a small war—almost forgotten now —did break out, between Italy and Turkey, over the possession of the Mediterranean seaport of Trieste. And before this "small" war could be ended, it had created the conditions for larger wars—the Balkan Wars of 1912-13. And before the Balkan Wars could be ended, they had created the conditions for one more war, the largest of them all—the great catastrophe of World War I.

In Prague, in 1911, Albert learned of another evil, an ancient one, that was beginning to reappear again. Among the Austrians in the city, he was told, there was a small band of men who were violently anti-Semitic. These Austrian anti-Semites said that the Jews were an inferior race—even "more inferior" than the Czecho-slovakians. They spread the same vicious lies that the Nazis were to spread fifteen and twenty years afterward. But this group was still small and without real power and so they kept their voices to a whisper.

Little by little during this period in his life, Albert began to feel a growing concern for the welfare of Europe's Jews. For a time he underestimated the forces of anti-Semitism, and thought that there was no serious danger in it. All the same, his indifference toward Jewish affairs was fast disappearing.

The more he learned about his fellow Jews, and about the difficulties which beset them, the deeper grew the bond linking him with the Jewish people.

During the year that he spent in Prague, Albert had

an assistant named Nohel, the son of a Jewish farmer. Young Nohel told Albert about the Jews who lived outside of Prague, how they tilled the soil around the little villages of Bohemia, and how they tried to save enough money to educate their sons. But, Nohel said, it was hard for most Jews in Bohemia to gain a higher education. He himself had been very fortunate. Few of Bohemia's Jews were allowed to enter the universities, where only the more favored races were welcome.

Young Nohel's words left a lasting impression on Albert's mind. It seemed more and more true to him that besides a common religious heritage, there was at least one trait, one passionate instinct, that united many of the Jews of Europe. This was their desire to become educated. To search after the truth, in science, in history, in art or literature, it didn't matter where one searched, it was the effort itself that was important.

There was a group of Czechoslovakian artists and writers in the city at this time, many of them Jewish, and Albert soon numbered them among his friends. One of this group was a dark, serious young man named Franz Kafka, who afterward became one of the most famous novelists of the century.

Some of these artists and writers were also early Zionists. They were not interested in politics, they did not believe in the importance of Palestine as a Jewish homeland, but rather they wished to make the Jews of central Europe proud of their religious and cultural heritage.

They believed it was a mistake for the Jews of Europe to try to become exactly like other Europeans, to try and assimilate themselves and lose their special identity.

Albert listened to their arguments, but took no active part in their program. He was still too concerned with his own work, too much absorbed in his own ideas to be willing to spend a great deal of energy on other activities.

Life in Prague was not all work and serious discussions for Albert. At the German University, he found a number of incidents that were amusing and that brought a smile to his lips. Once there was a question of his uniform. He was told that he had to buy a very special and fancy one, and that he had to wear it the first day of the term, when he was introduced to the other professors.

When would he have to wear it again? Albert asked. Never, he was told, unless he was granted the extraordinary privilege of meeting the Emperor of Austria himself, old Franz Joseph. *Must* he buy the uniform? Albert asked. Yes, it was the rule, he was told.

So he bought a uniform, and wore it the first day of the term, and then hung it away at the back of his closet. He never did meet the Emperor, and this was the only official time that he wore it.

Another thing that amused him at first, was the way that a new professor was supposed to pay his respects to all the other professors on the staff by going to their homes, one by one, and staying for afternoon tea. Albert used this custom as an excuse to walk through the old parts of the city, where there were some rare and lovely houses which interested him. But after a few weeks, he grew tired of pointless conversations and the rattle of teacups, and he stopped paying visits halfway down the list.

The professors who didn't receive a visit were very put out, until it was explained to them that young Professor Einstein was a bit "eccentric," and had only gone to tea in the first place because he had wanted to look at certain houses along the way. The professors were told that Albert's neglect was completely impersonal—he would have visited them instead, if they had lived on a different street.

By now, Albert's fame was beginning to spread. His name was well-known in scientific circles, and even newspapers and magazines in Europe and America were printing articles about him and about the theory of relativity which, according to the popular story, only four or five people in the entire world could understand.

Albert was still working furiously to improve and enlarge the theory. And in Prague, in 1911, he pointed out that the theory, which had never been subject to proof, might at last be tested.

In the autumn of 1914, he said, a full eclipse of the sun would be visible in parts of Russia. At that time, the sun would be dark for a few brief moments. It would then be possible to take photographs through a telescope of certain stars that seemed very close to the sun when seen from the earth. If the theory of relativity was true, Albert said, these stars would not be exactly where everyone thought they were. They would be a tiny distance off in another direction. He wrote down exactly where he was sure they would be in the photographs.

Nineteen fourteen was three years away, but soon the whole scientific world was stirring with excitement. Scientists were still divided into two camps, those who believed in the theory, and those who insisted that Einstein was either a madman or a fraud. Each year, though, it was growing harder to find an important mathematician or physicist who did not believe in the value of at least some of Albert's ideas.

When he had been in Prague only a few months, Albert's growing reputation brought him another offer, this time from the Polytechnical School in Zurich, where he had been a student less than a dozen years before. The professorship they offered him was a very fine one, and Mileva was anxious to return to Zurich. Albert told the professors at Prague that he would leave their university at the end of the year.

A few days before he left with his family, one of his sons asked him for a special favor. They had never taken a walk together while his father was wearing the wonderful uniform that still hung in the back of the closet. Would his father wear it outside, just once, before getting rid of it? Could they walk together through Prague, his father all dressed up in shiny gold braid, with a sword at his side, and a great three-cornered hat on his head?

It was the second and last time that Albert wore the uniform. With a good-humored twinkle in his eyes, he pulled on the trousers and coat, and with the help of his son, fixed the sword in place. And together they went out on the boulevards that day, the son bursting with pride at the sight of his father, and Albert smiling to himself and thinking, "Why, I look exactly like an admiral in the Brazilian Navy."

If Albert had been a proud or an ambitious man, his return to Zurich would have been an endless delight to him. In only a few years, his circumstances had changed completely. Wearing a good suit of clothes, he walked along the streets where he had once walked in a tattered suit and a frayed shirt. With a full meal inside his stomach, he passed the grimy restaurants where he had once eaten cheap and unwholesome food—when, indeed, he had eaten any food at all. And now, with his brief case in his hand, he walked up to the lecture desk at the Polytechnical School and looked down at his students, seated where he himself had often sat not many years before.

But he was neither a proud nor an ambitious man, and the importance of his position, the honors that were beginning to come to him, meant very little to his sense of happiness.

He was not a vengeful man either, and so, when he passed certain of his fellow professors in the halls and they bowed to him respectfully, these same narrow-minded men who had treated him so shamefully, who had refused to help him when he had been without money and was desperate for a job, when he passed them now, he returned their respectful bows without a smile of triumph or a hint of bitterness.

For truthfully, he no longer felt the slightest bitterness against them. What if they had once treated him badly? That was long since past. There was no point in dwelling on old wrongs. He had won out in spite of them. They had not prevented him from earning a living, and more important, they had not been able to silence him, to keep his thoughts from being published and from reaching the world.

Years after this, he received a letter from a girl in Holland, who complained of the way that her teachers were treating her. Albert answered that she should forget her grievances, as he had once forgotten his. "I suffered," he wrote to her, "at the hands of my teachers a similar treatment; they disliked me for my independence and passed me over when they wanted assistants. . . . But . . . one always cuts a poor figure when one complains about others who are struggling for their place in the sun too, after their own fashion. . . ."

This was why Albert forgave his teachers—because he knew that like most men they suffered from ambition, from the need to be respected, and that in their hunger for respect, they were sometimes forced, even against their better instincts, to act wrongly. Albert had learned, perhaps from his own past sufferings, to feel compassion for the weak-willed and the tempted, as well as for the innocent and the wronged.

By now there was no doubt that the theory of relativity was being widely studied, and if it was still not generally understood, at least its creator was considered a brilliant and original thinker.

As evidence of this, a few months after his return to Zurich, Albert received a new invitation. It was an astonishing one—so great an honor that at first he could scarcely believe that it had been offered to him.

One day in Zurich he was visited by two of Germany's leading scientists, Max Planck and Walter Nernst. They had been sent from Berlin, they told him, at the request of the President of the Kaiser Wilhelm Institute. They were empowered to offer Albert a permanent appointment as Professor at the Institute. In addition, Albert was offered membership in the Royal Prussian Academy of Science at a very handsome salary. This was the highest academic honor there was in Germany. Many outstanding professors at the University of Berlin never became members of the Prussian Academy.

Albert, they said, would have a lifetime appointment —not as a teaching professor, but as a professor extraordinary. He would not be required to teach regular courses, but could do what he wished, deliver a lecture whenever he pleased, and spend the rest of his time on his own ideas and theories.

Most of the members of the Prussian Academy were at least in their fifties. Albert was turning thirty-four. He would be the youngest member there. His own work would benefit from exchanging ideas with other members. And he would have complete freedom at last, no lectures to prepare, no examinations to correct, no administrative duties.

It was a dream come true—the dream that he had never allowed himself to have since that day, so many years before, when he had realized that his father was a poor man and that he himself, far from having a life of freedom and leisure, would have to struggle hard for his very existence.

A dream come true, yet at first, Albert did not accept the invitation. As much as he wished for freedom to pursue his ideas, he was unwilling to purchase that freedom except on his own terms.

The Prussian Academy had one rule that upset Albert very much. The more he thought about it, the more he became convinced that he could not conform to it. The Academy expected that its members would be German citizens. At last he wrote to Berlin and thanked the professors for the honor they had done him—he said he would have liked to accept the position—but that he could not if, in order to do so, he would have to give up his Swiss citizenship and become a German.

The Prussian Academy and the Kaiser Wilhelm Institute wanted to have Albert as a member. His fame was growing greater, month by month. The importance of his work was accepted almost everywhere—they *had* to have the brilliant young Dr. Einstein.

Fortunately, they discovered that an exception to the rule had already been made once before. A famous French scholar had become a member, without giving up his French citizenship.

"Yes, you can certainly remain a Swiss citizen if you choose to," they wrote to Albert. And he answered that he would be honored then to accept the position of professor in Berlin.

In 1913, Albert left Zurich, and took the train to Germany. It should have been a day of great rejoicing, but it was just the opposite, because he went alone.

Mileva and their two sons stayed behind in Zurich. She and Albert had decided to separate and get a divorce. There was no ill feeling between them, only the sad knowledge that they couldn't make each other happy, and that they were really better off apart.

Once before, Albert had gone to a railway station alone, a suitcase with all his possessions in one hand, his violin case in the other; only the first time, when he had taken the train to Milan as a youth of sixteen, he was returning to his family, to the people he loved. Now he was leaving his loved ones behind. And as he climbed on the train in Zurich, someone who recognized him said that his footsteps were heavy and that the tears were openly running down his cheeks.

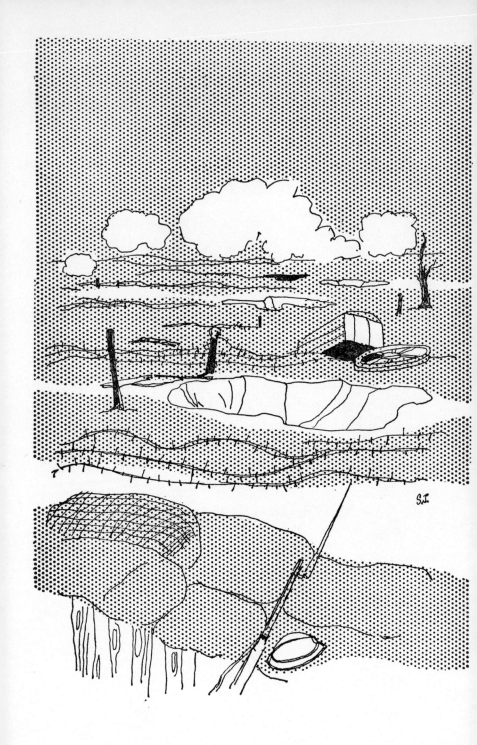

9

In 1913, when he was just thirty-four years old and at the height of his creative powers, Albert arrived in Berlin and took his place at the Kaiser Wilhelm Institute and at the Prussian Academy of Science.

He was treated with great respect by his fellow professors. His name was familiar to everyone, and whenever he gave one of his lectures, the room was always filled with an eager, attentive audience. His salary was far larger than he needed for himself, even after he had sent a generous sum to Switzerland to Mileva and their two children. He had a position of eminence, he had money, acclaim, yet in his heart he was far from certain that he had made a wise choice in returning to Germany.

The atmosphere in Berlin in 1913 was feverish and unsettled. There were so many soldiers marching in the streets, so many fifes and drums being played, so many steel helmets and steel bayonets flashing in the sun. Seeing these parading soldiers, Albert was often carried back to Munich, to his earliest childhood memories, and to his old feelings of horror and dismay at the warlike spirit of the people around him.

At the Academy itself, he found a number of professors who were extremely nationalistic, who believed in the superiority of the German race and in the right of Germany to enlarge her territories wherever she could. He detected among them that familiar German state of mind, the love of power and the desire to rule others, and along with it, the familiar disease of anti-Semitism, so shocking when found in men of great intellectual and cultural achievements.

Anti-Semitism, Albert knew, had existed in Germany for centuries, but before the rise of Bismarck and the Prussian "Junkers," it had never been strong in the German universities. If, he thought, the best-educated men in the country have anti-Semitic feelings, how much hope can there be of finding tolerance and good will among the ignorant, the superstitious, the uninformed? It was not, he realized, a very hopeful sign for the future of Germany.

Soon after his arrival in Berlin, his spirits were raised though, by a very pleasant surprise. He was invited to the apartment of one of his many uncles, a wealthy business man, and here he met Elsa, his cousin, whom he hadn't seen since the time when they had been children together in Munich, twenty or twenty-five years before. She was the little girl who had gone with him and Maya on so many of the Einstein family picnics to the lakes, and to the banks of the Isar River.

From their first night together in Berlin, he and Elsa got along wonderfully well. She was a small, friendly woman, with a sense of humor as quick as his own, and with a warm and generous disposition. He learned that she lived with her two young daughters, the children of a previous marriage.

Albert and Elsa sat on the sofa and talked with pleasure of the "old days" in Munich. Elsa asked him if he still played the violin? Albert told her that he certainly did —and then, seeing her smile, he added quickly that he had studied hard and practiced often, so that he hoped not quite so many ugly squeaks came out as the last time she had heard him play.

Albert became a regular visitor at his uncle's apartment. He told Elsa that he was amused by the way he was being received by his Berlin relatives. Years before, when he had been a struggling young man scarcely able to support himself, some of his more prosperous aunts and uncles had looked on him as the black sheep of the family. Now they seemed to be astonished at how "important" he had become, with his title of "Herr Professor" and his position at the Academy, and with his name mentioned from time to time in the newspapers. Clearly they no longer thought he was the black sheep, and so they welcomed him back to the family circle and gave him a place of honor and respect. Elsa shared Albert's amusement—they often looked at such things in the same way. It drew them together, and made them realize how pleasant and comfortable they felt, how much at ease in each other's company.

Nobody in the family was surprised when Elsa and Albert announced their plans to be married as soon as his divorce became final. The family smiled its approval, and more important, Elsa's two daughters, Ilse and Margot, already were very fond of him, and were happy at the idea that he would become their stepfather.

While Albert was finding unlooked-for happiness with Elsa, a happiness that would last and grow stronger through many years to come, the world around him was suddenly thrown into fear and confusion. A Serbian patriot shot and killed Archduke Ferdinand, the nephew of the Austrian Emperor and heir to the Austrian throne. For weeks afterward, during the long summer of 1914, peace hung by a few slender threads. Then, one by one, these threads snapped, and almost overnight, most of Europe was plunged into war.

In Berlin, Albert saw the most astonishing events. One day he watched a huge crowd assemble before the Royal Palace to demand that war be prevented. The very next day, he watched an even greater crowd assemble, to cheer the Emperor and the Army and the glorious war against the enemies of Germany.

What had changed the minds of the people? And why were they now willing, eager. to shed blood?

Flags hung out over the boulevards that afternoon, and men and women, laughing and shouting, rushed through the parks and streets. It was a city gone mad, in a world that had gone mad, too.

And Albert thought, yes, they are happy today, because at last they will no longer have to think for themselves. From now on, they will take orders from above, they will be told what their duty is and they will obey—and that really is all that they have ever been trained to do.

The beginning of the war brought a personal disappointment to Albert that would have greatly upset a less patient man. Only a few weeks before, a German scientific expedition had gone to Russia to photograph the eclipse of the sun, in order to prove or disprove what Albert had said in the Special Theory of Relativity and in some of his later work. But now Russia and Germany were enemies, and the German scientists on the expedition were arrested by the Russians and put in a prison camp. The eclipse of the sun went unphotographed, and Albert's work had to remain untested for a number of years longer.

At first, the war was very popular in Germany. The newspapers were controlled by the government, and printed only favorable news. In the west, the papers said, the German armies were approaching Paris, and soon the French government would be eager to sue for peace. At sea, the German Navy stood ready to challenge the might of the British Navy itself. In the east, the Russian armies of the Tsar were being successfully held in check.

But then the advance on Paris began to slow, and finally it ground to a stop at the Battle of the Marne. Afterward, there was a stalemate, and the beginning of four years of bitter trench warfare.

By the end of 1914, it was clear that the allied armies had escaped defeat, that the French government had no intention of suing for peace, and that the war might prove to be a great deal more painful and costly than had seemed likely the first few weeks of autumn in Berlin.

As the war went on, many things in Germany began to change, and life for Albert began to change, too. Years before, as a youth in Munich, he had often felt himself set apart, because of his pacifist beliefs, from the people of the city, his classmates, and even from his own family. Now, in Berlin, these same beliefs set him apart again.

At the outbreak of the war, Germany had invaded her neighbor, Belgium, despite a treaty that Germany had previously signed, guaranteeing Belgian neutrality. The world was shocked at such callousness and deceit; to make matters worse for the German government, rumors were spread by the English and French that German troops were committing thousands of unspeakable atrocities on defenseless Belgian civilians.

How, the world asked, could the country that had produced Beethoven and Goethe, the country whose musical and scientific achievements were the admiration and envy of all Europe, act in such a brutal way? How could it violate its treaties, invade neutral countries, and kill and maim innocent women and children? Surely civilized men in Germany, especially German scientists and artists, did not support the Emperor and his barbarian hordes.

To defend itself in the eyes of public opinion, the German government claimed that it had broken treaties only in self-defense, denied that German troops had committed atrocities, and insisted that all German scientists and artists supported the Emperor and his armies. To prove the last, ninety-two of Germany's leading scientists and artists signed a public paper, stating that they *did* support the Emperor completely. Only three men who were asked to sign refused to. Albert was one of the three.

From that day on, many of the professors at the Academy considered Albert to be almost a traitor. At official meetings, no one would sit next to him, so that on either side he always had an empty chair. They stopped exchanging social calls with him, and did their best to cut him off from all of the public activities of the Academy.

It was fortunate for Albert that he had kept his Swiss citizenship when he had returned to Germany two years before. The German government had little authority over him, since he was officially a citizen of a neutral country, and not legally a German at all.

When he insisted on speaking out and stating his opinions—as he did more and more strongly, no matter what personal risk he ran—the government could not do much to harm him. Had he become a German citizen, though, he would have faced serious charges, and would probably have spent several years in jail.

As the war continued, a number of military and technical problems arose, and the country's scientists, especially chemists and physicists, were called on to help solve them.

Walter Nernst, who had done so much to bring Albert to Berlin, devoted himself to the development of new and more efficient types of poison gas. Fritz Haber, a close friend of Albert's, developed new chemicals necessary to the manufacturing of munitions. Other scientists worked on ways to improve weather forecasting, wireless transmission, submersion and detection devices for submarines in the German Navy, submarines which were bringing death to thousands by sinking unarmed merchantmen and passenger ships.

Albert refused to take part in any of this war work. Instead, he began to devote his energies to the cause of peace.

He became a member of almost every anti-war group in Germany, and before long, he was known as one of the leading pacifists in the country. He signed a petition, denouncing Germany's attack on Belgium, which was published shortly after the paper praising the Emperor, which the ninety-two scientists and artists had signed.

He helped organize a pacifist group, the "Union of the New Fatherland," which boldly demanded an immediate end to the war. Few men had the courage to support such an unpopular cause. The "Union" never gained many members. In 1915, it was ordered to disband by the government.

Albert had known from the start that little practical good would come of its activities. The German people didn't want peace yet. But Albert didn't care about *that*, he had to speak the truth, even if, in doing so, he risked his own safety. War was wrong, the greatest of crimes, and he had to do what he could to keep this fact constantly in front of the German people.

His pacifist beliefs brought him the friendship of Romain Rolland, a famous French novelist, who worked in France, all during the course of the war, to help the cause of peace.

They met in Switzerland in 1915, while Albert was on a holiday, visiting his two sons. What Rolland wrote in his notebook after their meeting showed that Albert was surprisingly sensitive to the true nature of the war and its consequences.

Albert told Rolland two things: that it would be impossible to conclude a lasting peace with Germany unless Germany were defeated first, and that no matter which side finally "won" the war, the real loser would be France.

Both predictions eventually proved true. And they proved that Albert, who had once thought that he could live alone in a world of his own ideas, had long since changed his mind. He was already an intelligent judge of public events; soon, he would be called on to take part in some of them.

10

For four terrible years, World War I continued to rage in Europe, with neither side able to defeat the other. German victories over the Russians on the Eastern Front were balanced by the failure of the German Army to advance in the west. French and English soldiers still held the trenches barring the way to Paris. Worst of all, for the German cause, the English Navy still controlled the seas.

Using its many warships, England established a blockade around Germany. Supplies of all kinds were cut off; food became scarce, and millions of Germans, many of them innocent school children, began to suffer from slow starvation.

In Berlin, Albert was spared the worst of this physical suffering, but he did not escape unharmed. His stomach had never been strong since his student days in Zurich, and now the unwholesome food that he ate—when he remembered to eat regular meals at all—only made his old condition worse.

Friends who saw him in Switzerland on one of his frequent trips there were shocked at his appearance. He had lost sixty pounds. His health, perhaps his life, was in danger.

They begged him not to return to Germany after his holiday. "It could kill you," they said. "If you won't stay here for your own sake, do it for ours. You owe it to your friends to save what's left of your health."

But Albert could be very stubborn—it was perhaps the most serious fault in his character. And he had already made up his mind that his work for peace and his scientific studies had to be carried on inside Germany. And back he went, despite their protests.

It was fortunate that his divorce had become final by then, and that he and Elsa were married soon afterward. This second marriage may have helped to save his life.

Elsa saw how weak he was growing, and she did her utmost to preserve his remaining strength. She was an excellent cook, and three times a day she saw to it that he ate a wholesome, filling meal in their apartment, instead of allowing him to follow his old bachelor habit of snatching food whenever the thought struck him, and in any chance restaurant that happened to catch his eye.

Luckily, too, she and Albert had a number of generous friends and relatives in neutral Switzerland, where, because there was no blockade, food was still plentiful. Albert and Elsa received many food packages from Switzerland, and with the help of these, she was able to prepare better meals for him than the ones he had been eating before. Soon he had stopped losing weight, and the worst of his illness was over.

Their marriage was fortunate for Albert in other ways. It brought an end to the loneliness that he had felt after his separation from Mileva and his two sons, and it gave him a new family at a time when he needed the warmth of family life. He had always loved children, and soon he felt that little Ilse and Margot were as dear to him as his own boys.

Elsa was a very kind and understanding woman. She knew that Albert occasionally had moods of depression, and she tried to accept them patiently and without complaint.

Sometimes, in the evening, Albert withdrew into himself, picked up his violin, and playing softly, soothed the sad feelings that swelled up in his heart. Then Elsa and the two girls would listen quietly until the music was over, and the look of sorrow had passed from his face.

At other times, when he felt more cheerful, she and the two girls would sit with him in the living room and talk about the latest happenings in their lives—the shortage of meat at the butcher's that week, a neighbor who had just returned the pipe tobacco he had borrowed from Albert, a cousin of theirs who had unexpectedly returned home on leave from the Army.

These simple, commonplace hours were a source of great comfort to Albert; for a while they took his thoughts away from the daily newspapers with their endless stories of the war, and from the burden of his own scientific work, which he had continued to develop, painstakingly, step by step, despite the many difficulties of life in wartime Berlin.

Since 1905, when the Special Theory had first appeared, Albert had been working on a new theory of relativity that would include not only the Special Theory but many previously undreamed of ideas about the nature of the universe.

In 1916, with the war still going on, the General Theory of Relativity was published. It was even more difficult to understand than the Special Theory had been. It used many complicated equations that only highly skilled mathematicians could interpret.

It was much more original, much more "revolutionary" then the Special Theory. It said that the old physics of Isaac Newton which had been taught for three hundred years was not really able to explain the true nature of the universe. It said, among other things, that space was "curved"—that a ray of light, for instance, instead of traveling in a straight line forever, might eventually return to the point where it had started from.

Among scientists and mathematicians, there were two reactions. One group of men held out against Albert's theory because it made some of the work that they had done seem unimportant, even meaningless. And they were afraid of new and complicated ideas. They wanted to continue to believe in "pre-Einstein" physics, in the physics of Newton, because they understood and could explain Newton's ideas, and they were almost completely baffled by Albert's.

The second group read Albert's long, sixty-four-page paper which contained the General Theory, and felt awe and amazement. They knew that this was a great achievement by the greatest thinker among them; and they knew that if what the General Theory said was true, it was one of the most magnificent achievements in the history of human thought.

Albert himself fully realized what he had done. He was pleased that his work had turned out so well, and humbled at the knowledge that he had been fortunate enough to contribute something beautiful and permanent to mankind's understanding of nature and the universe.

Once, Leopold Infeld, a fellow scientist who often worked with Albert, said that he thought the Special Theory might have been developed in another few years by somebody else, even if Albert had not developed it himself.

Albert cheerfully agreed. From what other scientists

had done before 1900, the Special Theory *had* to be developed. "But," he said, "this is not true of the General Theory of Relativity. I doubt whether it would have been known even yet."

In England, in 1917, Sir Arthur Eddington, a member of the Royal Astronomical Society, studied the General Theory, and soon realized its significance. Sir Arthur was a great astronomer, and one of the few men in the world who could understand Albert's ideas. He noted two things: Albert's suggestion that the theory could be tested by photographing a full eclipse of the sun, and the fact that in 1919, such an eclipse would next take place.

Sir Arthur brought the matter to the attention of the Royal Society. At first the other members were openly hostile. Albert Einstein?—he was a *German*, wasn't he?—at least he had been born in Germany and he lived there now, and this certainly meant that he was German enough, the members said. No thank you, they were not interested in Einstein and his theory. Anything German, anything that was in any way connected with the Enemy, even German scientific ideas, were of no concern to decent, peace-loving, patriotic English astronomers.

Sir Arthur patiently argued the importance of the theory, the need for better understanding between nations, and the important role that men of science could take in leading the world back to peace and sanity. After a long debate, the other astronomers overcame their feelings of hatred for all things German, and it was finally agreed that if the Society possibly could, it would send out some of its members to photograph the eclipse of 1919.

But that was still two years in the future, and in 1917 such a plan did not seem to have much chance of success. The Royal Society could not hope to send out scientific expeditions while the war was still going on, and the war showed no sign of ending.

There were new victories for both sides, but none was decisive. The Communist Revolution had swept over Russia, and the Russian armies, already badly defeated by the Germans, withdrew from the fighting in 1917. In November, at the Battle of Caporetto in the south, the Italians suffered a tremendous defeat at the hands of the Germans and the Austrians.

On the other hand, Germany's submarine campaign and the sinking of neutral ships had finally brought America into the war. By late 1917, American supplies of food and munitions were pouring into France, along with the first American soldiers, unwearied by three years of fighting.

The entrance of America into the war ended the balance of strength between Germany and her enemies.

Blockaded by the English Navy, cut off from raw materials and food supplies, Germany grew weaker while the Allies grew stronger.

But inside Germany, only the ruling classes, the Prussian "Junkers" and the high military officers, had any chance of knowing how completely desperate the situation really was. The newspapers still talked of victory, when victory was no longer possible. They talked of the spring campaign that would crush the Allied armies and end in the capture of Paris. There was scant mention of the actual number of German soldiers dead, wounded, missing, of the serious lack of guns and ammunition and troops.

In the spring of 1918, like a great wounded animal, the German armies struck in the west for the last time. Across French soil, where so much of the war had been fought, their gray companies and battalions attacked, driving the Allied soldiers slowly before them. In July, at the Second Battle of the Marne, they were halted again, still miles short of Paris.

The war dragged on cruelly for four months longer. The German armies, as exhausted as the country itself, began to retreat, all hope of victory gone. Still the German government refused to surrender. Still the newspapers tried to hide the truth from the desperate, half-starved German people.

But the people and soldiers had suffered as long as

they could. There were protest marches in the cities, food riots, crowds marching with placards calling for an armistice and an end to fighting.

Then, with incredible swiftness, the German government collapsed. Emperor William II abdicated his throne and fled to Holland, and on the 11th of November, 1918, the great war came to an end.

A new government was quickly formed in Berlin, by men who were not soldiers or Prussian aristocrats, but socialists and liberals. Albert was pleased that for the first time in its brief history, Germany would not be ruled by men who believed in armed might and conquest.

And he would scarcely have been human had he not also been pleased that the Royal Society had decided to send out two expeditions the following year, one to Brazil and one to Africa, to photograph the next eclipse of the sun.

The reason that two expeditions were sent out was this: a full eclipse of the sun lasts only four or five minutes, and if, during that brief time, clouds come between the earth and the sun, any photographs taken may prove to be worthless. So the astronomers of the Society decided to increase their chance of success by having photographic teams in two widely separated places.

Sir Arthur Eddington headed the expedition that sailed to the island of Principe in the Gulf of Guinea,

West Africa. He arrived with his team a month before the eclipse, and, with his fellow astronomers, studied the countryside and arranged to set up his cameras.

As the day of the eclipse drew near, excitement rose higher and higher in the camp. The main question in everyone's mind was the weather—would it be favorable or not? If it rained, or even if there were thick clouds, the months of preparation, the money spent, the trip to Africa, all would be wasted. There would be no photograph of the darkened sun and the nearby stars, and no way to tell if Albert's theory of relativity were true or not.

Early on the morning of the eclipse, Sir Arthur arose to a discouraging sight. The sky was partly overcast, with broken cloudbanks in all directions.

There was no help for the unfavorable weather. Perhaps, when the eclipse began, the clouds would not completely conceal the sun. There was still a slim chance of success.

Gradually the eclipse began, the moon passing between the earth and the sun, the sun gradually becoming hidden until its entire surface was dark, and the corona, formed by flames on the sun's outer edge, became visible.

Quickly, carefully, in the eerie half-light, for the five minutes and two seconds of the total eclipse, Sir Arthur and his team took photographs, sixteen of them, through the passing clouds. Then, with mounting impatience, they developed the photographs.

In fifteen, one or more important stars were hidden by clouds. All fifteen were worthless. In the sixteenth, five important stars were visible—and they were enough.

Sir Arthur and his expedition sailed back to England with all speed, to compare this one photograph with other photographs taken in England of the same five stars. According to Albert's prediction, the stars in Sir Arthur's photograph would not be in the same place in relation to the sun as they were in the English photographs.

When Sir Arthur compared them, he found that this was true. The stars had moved away from the sun and were almost exactly where Albert had said they would be.

On the 7th of November, 1919, the Royal Society announced their findings in the London newspapers. Albert's theory was true, his ideas about the universe had taken the place of Isaac Newton's. Word of his achievement leaped around the world. And Albert Einstein, whose work was so complicated that most scientists couldn't understand it, became a popular hero overnight.

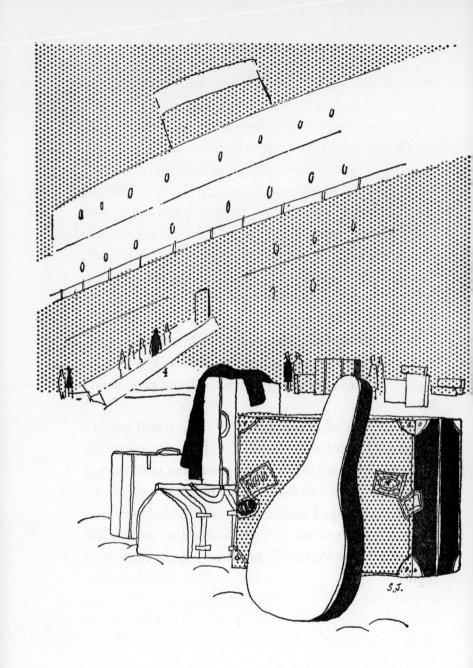

S.J.

11

Part of the price of fame, as Albert soon discovered, is the loss of privacy. A famous man must expect to remain in the spotlight, to meet newspapermen everywhere and to be asked many questions.

Just twenty-four hours after Sir Arthur Eddington's announcement that Albert's prophecies had been proved correct, the first newspaper reporter came to the Einstein apartment at 5 Haberlandstrasse, in Berlin.

He was from *The London Times*, he said, and he asked Albert to explain, if he would, a little about "relativity" for English readers.

Albert was quite willing to do so. He was always glad of the chance to talk about his ideas, in the hope that he might be able to make them seem less mysterious to men and women who were not trained scientists or mathematicians. He gave a brief explanation of his theory, and then he had another thought.

Could he say something, he wondered, to this Eng-

lish reporter—and through the reporter, to the English
people—which might help to lessen the hatred that so
many Englishmen still felt for Germany? Yes, he decided, he certainly could. It was the first time he used
his new "fame" in this good cause, but it was not the
last time that he did so.

"It is quite in keeping," Albert told the English reporter that day, "with the great and proud traditions of
scientific work in your country, that eminent men of research should devote time and effort to examine the re-
sults of a theory published during the war in the country of your enemies. Without my English colleagues, I
would never have received in my lifetime the proof of
the most important development of my theory."

Albert's message was a gesture of good will, a small
attempt to bring the former enemy nations closer together. The establishment of understanding and friendship between Germany and her conquerors was one of
Albert's deepest wishes, and for years he did everything
in his power to help heal the scars left by the war.

From the day when the first reporter arrived at No. 5,
Haberlandstrasse, life was never quite the same again for
Albert and Elsa. Soon, more reporters began to arrive,
and they asked more questions.

They asked Albert about relativity, and they asked
him about himself. When did he usually work on his
theories?—in the mornings, the afternoons—and where

did he work?—and what did he eat?—and how much did he smoke?—and what were his hobbies?—on and on, an endless stream of questions, which, the reporters explained, would tell the people of the world what they wanted to know about Albert Einstein, the "father of relativity."

At first, Albert was sure that all this fuss was only temporary. "After all," he said to Elsa, "it can't last long." It wasn't possible, he believed, for a scientist like himself to interest people the way a championship prize-fighter or a topflight football player interested them. But still the reporters came and asked their questions, and then the photographers set up their cameras and took his picture, and soon his face began to appear in dozens of newspapers and magazines.

Albert was totally unprepared for so much excitement and publicity. Only gradually did he finally come to realize how completely his theory had caught the imagination of the public. For although hardly anyone understood what his theory really said, most people accepted it on faith as a kind of "miracle," and were eager to learn as much as they could about the "great Professor Einstein."

And slowly Albert began to see that because of "relativity," his name and his face were now public property, and that whatever he said or did would be a matter of importance to thousands and even millions of people.

Elsa found, to her astonishment, that she too was now in the public eye. She often had her picture taken with Albert, and she also was interviewed by reporters and was asked all kinds of questions.

What was it like to be married to a genius? Did Albert usually discuss his work with her? Did she really understand relativity, or was she as much in the dark as everyone else? Would she advise other women to marry a genius if they could, or did she think that a man of average intelligence made a more satisfactory husband?

Elsa, who was even shyer than Albert, suffered secret agonies when she had to appear in public and answer the questions of the curious, or assume the part of a famous man's wife. But she had no choice—Albert *was* famous now, and these were things that the whole world expected of her. Besides, the more questions she answered and the more reporters she talked with, the more chance Albert had to escape from the spotlight to the privacy and peace which he needed so much.

Before long, dozens of letters began to arrive at the Einstein apartment, and usually it was Elsa who had to answer them. They contained invitations to banquets and luncheons and teas. If Albert had gone to only a tenth of them, he would never have had time to do anything else.

Other letters came from cranks and even madmen,

asking for Albert's help in promoting their wild and insane schemes. There were still other letters, containing offers of money if Albert would endorse certain products or appear at gatherings and deliver speeches. Once, there was a letter from Hollywood, from a famous producer, who said that he would be delighted to pay a huge sum of money for the exclusive movie rights to "The Life of Albert Einstein."

Patiently, with Albert's advice, Elsa answered all these letters, refusing most of the invitations, turning away the cranks and madmen, rejecting the offers of money.

And still more letters came—some of them simple and touching. A number of parents wrote to say that they had just named their newborn son "Albert" in honor of the great scientist. Others wrote asking for money and telling harrowing stories of personal misfortune. To these, Albert responded with whatever small sums he could afford. And a number of people, especially students, wrote and asked for his help in furthering their careers.

Albert was struck by the fact that so many Jewish students wrote to him, from Germany and from various other European countries; they said that they had once hoped to enter a university to complete their studies, but that now, because they were Jewish, they were not allowed to do so.

The plight of Jewish students in Europe distressed Albert more and more. He remembered Nohel, his young assistant in Prague, and how Nohel had told him about the talented boys and girls in Bohemia who were kept out of the universities there because of anti-Semitism. From the letters that he continually received, Albert could see that discrimination against Jewish students was growing worse in Europe instead of better.

Jewish questions of all kinds began to interest him profoundly. He asked himself about his own position as a Jew, where he stood in relation to Judaism, and why the misfortunes of other Jews preyed so strongly on his feelings?

Sometimes he discussed these matters with his good friend, Walter Rathenau, a brilliant Jewish businessman, intellectual, and politician. During the war, Walter Rathenau had been given the almost impossible task of getting adequate supplies to the German armies, and his work had won the praise of the General Staff and of the Emperor himself. Now he was a member of the new government, which was called the "Weimar Republic." Before long he would become Germany's Foreign Minister, and would then hold the most important cabinet post in the government.

One day, as they talked, Walter Rathenau said something which struck a deep chord in Albert's mind, so that afterward, Albert couldn't forget his friend's words.

Rathenau said, "If a Jew were to tell me that he had gone hunting for pleasure, I would know one thing—he was telling me a lie!"

At first Albert laughed—until he saw what his friend was really suggesting—that Jews hate to shed blood because they have an ingrained respect for life in any form. The ideal that life is infinitely precious is an important Jewish ideal—and one in which Albert had always passionately believed.

Increasingly he felt the mysterious, intangible bonds which tied him to his people. A respect for life in all its forms, a yearning for knowledge and wisdom, a desire for personal independence—these things, Albert believed, were Jewish characteristics, were the essence of the Jewish spirit in any age and in any place—and they were also things which he prized highly himself. This Jewishness was a part of him—whether he willed it or not—as it was a part of all Jews, everywhere.

Ever since the end of the war, Albert had been attracted to Zionism, the struggle of the Jewish people to establish their own nation in Palestine, and now he formed a close friendship with Chaim Weizmann, the great Zionist leader.

Dr. Weizmann was also a scientist. During the war, he had lived in England, and his work as a research chemist had been of tremendous help to the English government. Because of this help, Dr. Weizmann had been able to meet and talk with important Englishmen, and as a result of these talks, the English government finally promised the Jewish people a homeland in Palestine.

One evening, in 1921, Dr. Weizmann asked Albert if

he would be willing to use his growing fame to support the Zionist cause. In what way? Albert wanted to know. Well, would Albert be willing to accompany him to America in order to interest more of America's Jews in Zionism, and in order to raise money for the Jewish National Fund and especially for the Hebrew University, in Jerusalem?

Albert held back for a time, while he tried to decide whether or not to accompany Dr. Weizmann on such a trip. He was particularly worried lest any public action that he take have an important political effect inside Germany. He believed that the liberal Weimar Republic was the best government that Germany had ever had; earlier that same year, in order to express his faith in the new regime, he had given up his Swiss citizenship and had become a German again.

The Weimar Republic was not strong, though, and its enemies might now use Albert's support of Zionism as a weapon to attack both Jews and German liberals—and through them, to attack the government itself. If necessary, however, Albert finally decided this was a risk that would have to be run.

Because, as he knew only too well, there were vital reasons why he should support Zionism and Dr. Weizmann's efforts on behalf of the Jewish people.

A few months before, Albert had given a series of lectures in Prague. He had stayed with Professor Philipp Frank, who had succeeded Albert as professor of theoretical physics at the German University in Prague, in 1912. They were old friends, and Albert spoke freely to Professor Frank about the political situation in Germany.

Albert was already fearful of a "right-wing revolution"—the seizing of power by various fascist and anti-Semitic groups, who were even then forming themselves into the National Socialist Party—the Nazis. He told Professor Frank that he did not think that he would like to remain in Germany for more than ten years. By then, he believed, the Nazis would be in power, and all of Germany's Jews would be in grave danger. And when that evil time came, a Jewish nation, if it existed in Palestine, might prove a welcome haven to the Jews in Germany.

There were other vital reasons, Albert felt, why he should support Zionism. For a long time, too many Jews had ignored the fact, and had even attempted to deny, that there were such things as a Jewish life and a Jewish heritage. German Jews, especially, had turned their backs on their own history and culture, in the hope that they would be "accepted" by other Germans and fully assimilated into the German nation.

But this assimilation had not taken place. On the contrary, anti-Semitism in Germany was daily growing stronger and more widespread.

Even worse than this, Jews were beginning to turn against one another. When Polish and other Eastern

Jews arrived in Germany as refugees, the Jews in Germany often refused to help them, treated them as their inferiors, and denounced them publicly—in the hope that they, the German Jews, would gain the favor of other Germans and escape the effects of anti-Semitic feelings.

This was a completely heartless and a degrading thing for men to do. It was also a foolish way for the Jews of Germany to act, because it really gained them nothing. No matter what they said, no matter what they did, in the eyes of most Germans, they still remained Jews themselves.

This is how Albert once explained the matter: "However much the Jews adapted themselves, in language and manners . . . to the European peoples among whom they lived, the feeling of strangeness between the Jews and their hosts never disappeared. This spontaneous feeling is the ultimate cause of anti-Semitism, which is therefore not to be got rid of by well-meaning propaganda. Nationalities want to pursue their own path, not to blend. A satisfactory state of affairs can only be brought about by mutual toleration and respect."

And how could this mutual toleration and respect be gained by the Jews in Germany, in Europe, in the whole world? Albert went on to say this: "The first step is . . . that we Jews should once more become conscious of our existence as a nationality and regain the self-respect that is necessary to a healthy existence. We must learn once more to glory in our ancestors and our history and once again take upon ourselves, as a nation, cultural tasks of a sort calculated to strengthen our sense of the community. It is not enough for us to play a part as individuals in the cultural development of the human race; we must also tackle tasks which only nations as a whole can perform. Only so can the Jews regain social health."

Turning these thoughts over in his mind, Albert finally reached a decision. Each day, the need to bring the Jewish nation into being became more clear to him. And the work of the university in Palestine was of particular importance. It would be a place where Jewish students from all over the world could study and learn a profession, a university which they could attend without any feelings of inferiority and without being made objects of hatred and ridicule.

Yes, Albert said to Dr. Weizmann, he would join him on a trip to America with all his heart.

Albert put his hopes for the Jewish homeland in these few, simple words: "Palestine will be a center of culture for all Jews, a refuge for the most grievously oppressed, a field of action for the best among us, a unifying ideal, and a means of attaining inward health for the Jews of the whole world."

Before many weeks, he and Dr. Weizmann and their wives had left Germany, and were on their way to visit the new world.

12

In April 1921, when the S. S. *Rotterdam* arrived in New
York, an army of American news reporters was waiting at the pier to meet Albert Einstein, the most famous
scientist in the world. On the ship's deck, they found a
quiet, friendly man of medium height, whose black hair
was turning gray, and whose broad shoulders were a little stooped. Albert was dressed plainly, almost care-
lessly, in a worn raincoat and a black felt hat. In one
hand he carried his violin case, in the other, his pipe.

After dozens of questions, after dozens of photographs, Albert and Elsa and the Weizmanns were es-
corted from the ship and taken to City Hall, where
they were formally greeted by Mayor Hylan. Then
they returned to their open limousine, and were driven
through the city, in a giant parade that was held in Albert's honor.

Before he had come to New York, Albert was sure
that he had already experienced every kind of public ac-

claim—but he had not yet been treated to an American welcome. Thousands of people lined the streets of lower Manhattan and cheered and shouted greetings as his car drove by. Other thousands hung out of office windows and threw paper streamers and bits of confetti, until the entire avenue looked as though it had been struck by a blizzard. Overhead, airplanes roared in the sky. And at the head of the parade there was a gigantic poster with Albert's picture and the words: "This is the Famous Professor Einstein."

Everywhere that he went, Albert was greeted by huge crowds, eager to catch a glimpse of the scientist whose ideas and speculations had changed man's understanding of the universe. He was made welcome, and he enjoyed the experience—as much as he ever enjoyed appearing in public before large numbers of strangers. Afterward, when asked to describe his impression of Americans, he said that he had found them "friendly and self-confident." And, he added, he had learned that meeting Americans was "easy and agreeable."

Albert's first visit to America lasted less than two months, and he was busy almost every minute of it. Many of his days were spent with Dr. Weizmann. There were banquets and smaller gatherings where Dr. Weizmann spoke, explaining the problems besetting the Jews of Europe and the benefits which he believed a Jewish nation would bring to Jews of all countries, whether or not they chose to come to Palestine themselves.

Albert and Dr. Weizmann met with heartening success at these gatherings. Because of their appeals, a great deal of money was generously pledged by the Jews of America, to help new settlers build homes and cultivate untilled land in Palestine, and to help the provisional government establish industries so that men could find work and the country itself could become more self-sufficient.

At a meeting in Philadelphia, Jewish doctors were especially generous. Their gifts made it possible to start a medical school as part of the Hebrew University. Here, doctors could be trained, and many diseases, particularly those of the Middle East, could be studied, to insure the health of all peoples living in Palestine.

Between fund-raising efforts, Albert managed to deliver scientific lectures in New York City, both at Columbia University and at City College. Then he was taken to Washington, to the White House, to meet President Harding. Finally, a few days before his ship was to sail for Europe, Albert went to Princeton University to receive an honorary degree and to deliver a last series of lectures.

In awarding the degree, President Hibben said of Albert, "We salute the new Columbus of science, voyaging through strange seas of thought alone." It was an apt description of the solitary inner life that Albert had led for so many years.

Princeton University, Albert saw, was set in a charming, old-fashioned New Jersey town. The cherry trees and the dogwoods were just coming into blossom. Lawns looked fresh and green. The streets were quiet, deserted—a welcome change after the bustle and excitment of New York and Philadelphia and Washington.

Albert enjoyed his brief stay in Princeton. He felt drawn to the peaceful, sleepy town—and one day, a number of years later, he would have occasion to think of Princeton again, and to remember the pleasant impression it had made on him.

On their way back home to Berlin, Albert and Elsa stopped off in England where, for a few days, they were the house guests of Lord Haldane, an important English statesman. One evening, Lord Haldane gave a party for Albert. Among the diners were many of the leading political, scientific and artistic figures in England. George Bernard Shaw was there, Alfred North Whitehead, the famous philosopher, the Archbishop of Canterbury, and Sir Arthur Eddington, the astronomer who had worked so hard to help prove Albert's theories.

There seemed no end to the famous and influential people who wanted to meet Albert, yet he remained unaffected by the compliments and the honors that were being paid to him. Truthfully, he would have preferred to live quietly and unnoticed, but that was no longer possible.

Often, political considerations made it necessary for him to accept certain invitations. His friend Walter Rathenau had assured Albert that he was now a sort of "good-will ambassador" for Germany—and it was easy to see how badly Germany needed such an ambassador. In England and France, in fact, throughout much of the world, the very word "German" was still an object of intense hatred. And so Albert, realizing his unique ability to spread good will, accepted invitations that he would have refused had he been considering only his personal feelings.

Meeting so many influential people, he had the chance to speak up for unpopular or misunderstood ideals, and to gain support for them—for pacifism and disarmament, for the Zionist cause and the right of the Jewish people to settle in Palestine, for international co-operation and peace. And because he was recognized as a great man of science, his opinions on nonscientific subjects were also listened to with respect. His support of Zionism leant much strength and vigor to the movement, and his public utterances encouraged Jews everywhere in their struggle to help build a Jewish nation.

Albert made a remarkable impression on many of the wealthy people whom he visited from time to time, because of his simple tastes. When he arrived for a stay of

several days, carrying only his violin and one small suitcase, his host and hostess assumed that the rest of his
luggage had been delayed at the railroad station. It
wasn't possible, they thought, for the famous Professor
Einstein to bring only *one* suitcase on his visit. Even
when Albert explained that a single suitcase was enough
for his needs, they were invariably astonished, and
talked about his "eccentric behavior" long after his visit
was over.

He never learned to enjoy the wealth and pomp that
often surrounded him when he was away from home.
He loved simplicity, and was amused at the thought of
footmen and butlers and valets being assigned to wait on
a man like himself, who had absolutely no need of their
services.

Albert's indifference to luxury, and even to ordinary
personal comforts, sometimes caused great confusion
and anxiety to others. Only those who knew him inti-
mately realized that when he took a train—unless Elsa
had bought his ticket and put it into his pocket before-
hand—he would buy a third-class ticket because he saw
no reason to spend more money for a better seat. Several
times, his hosts, coming to the railroad station to meet
him, missed him completely—for it never occurred to
them that a famous man like Albert would ever travel in
a third-class railway carriage.

Back home again, after his first trip to America and
England, Albert found Berlin and all of Germany a very

depressing spectacle. Times were hard. Unemployment was high. Many businesses were failing. A heavy burden to the country were the huge sums of money demanded by France, to pay the damages that the German armies had done to French homes and farms and factories during the war.

In Germany, money itself began to lose its value. More and more paper money had to be printed. One day the mark might be worth ten cents, the next day only five. Though few people realized it, the country's monetary system was being manipulated by a few selfish industrialists for their own profit. While they grew even richer by purchasing factories and property for almost nothing, the average German found his pension reduced, his job gone, his life savings wiped out. Before the inflation was over, a housewife had to exchange a suitcaseful of paper money in order to buy a loaf of bread or a bit of cheese to feed her family.

In such circumstances, anti-Semitism flourished more openly. Members of the National Socialist Party—the Nazis—with their brown uniforms, their leather boots, their swastika arm bands, began to appear in the streets and to hold public meetings for the first time.

The Jews were responsible, they said, for all of Germany's ills. The Jews had secretly tricked the government into surrendering to France in 1918, just when the war—far from being lost—had actually been won. The Jews had treacherously stabbed Germany in the back.

The Jews had planned the armistice, and the Treaty of Versailles, with its huge sums of money that had to be paid to France. The Jews were to blame for everything.

Many middle-class Germans, ruined by the war and by post-war inflation, were willing to believe the Nazis and to support them. So were many ex-soldiers, discharged from the Army, unemployed, with neither the means to support themselves nor any real hope for the future. The easiest thing for these disillusioned, bitter, frustrated people to do was to find a scapegoat. When the Nazi rabble-rousers said "blame it on the Jews," many ordinary Germans were only too eager to follow their advice.

Because he was a pacifist, and a Jew, and the most honored living scientist, Albert soon became a special object of hatred to the Nazis and to other German nationalists and anti-Semites.

Among German scientists, there sprang up a Nazi group that attempted to discredit Albert's achievments. The leader of this group was Philipp Lenard, a skilled physicist and a former winner of the Nobel Prize. During the war he had become an extreme nationalist, and after the war he was an early and enthusiastic member of the Nazi Party. He hated Albert because he hated all Jews, and he was jealous of Albert because his own reputation was comparatively insignificant.

Lenard called Albert's theories "absurd," and tried to ridicule them, yet Lenard had one great difficulty—the formula, $E=MC^2$ had tremendous scientific value, and could not be ignored.

So, by unsound arguments and deliberate falsehoods, Lenard "proved" that $E=MC^2$ had not been developed by the "Jewish Einstein," but by an Austrian physicist, Friederich Hasenöhrl, who had been killed during the war while "patriotically serving in the Austrian Army." And with this difficulty solved, Lenard and other Nazi scientists were able to avoid mentioning Albert's name, and could, instead, talk of $E=MC^2$ as the "Principle of Hasenöhrl."

Albert was one of the first men in Germany to understand the extreme ruthlessness and depravity of the Nazis, and the danger that their expanding movement posed to any free and decent life in Germany. But even Albert was shocked by what happened in Berlin on the 24th of June, 1922.

It was a warm, early summer afternoon. Walter Rathenau, now the government's Foreign Minister, was driving through one of Berlin's parks. His car was approached by another car which had been waiting for him. There was a burst of gunfire and Rathenau slumped against the seat, dying in a welter of blood.

When his assassins were finally caught, they proved to be young Nazis, hardly out of their teens. Why had they killed Rathenau? At their trial they gave the reason —he was a Jew. To young Nazi thugs, that single fact was a sufficient excuse for killing anyone. Even a man like Walter Rathenau, a distinguished German patriot, who had done so much to help his country during the war.

Albert felt bitter grief at Rathenau's death, but he refused to take extra precautions for his own safety. What would be, would be—he desired no protection from the police, though he knew that the Nazis hated him almost as much as they had hated his friend.

For Elsa, the assassination meant terrible days of fear and uncertainty. It was she who went to the police, though Albert was never aware of this, and arranged for his protection. When he left for Holland, where he went to spend several months, the railroad station in Berlin was teeming with detectives. Two of them, posing as businessmen, got into Albert's compartment and rode with him all the way to his destination, to be sure that he arrived safely.

Elsa's peace of mind was not helped by a rumor that swept through Berlin; the rumor said that in searching for the assassins, a list of future victims had been found, and that Albert's name was prominent on the list.

On his return from Holland, she urged Albert to leave Germany again, to go anywhere, until conditons in the country became calmer. And it was with a sense of relief that she learned one day of an invitation from Japan— they wanted Albert to deliver some lectures there.

Should the two of them go to Japan? he asked her, a good-natured twinkle in his eye.

Elsa didn't need to be asked twice. She started packing, and only when the German border was behind them, and their train was running swiftly south through France, did she relax and smile and believe that Albert was really out of danger.

13

Their voyage to the Middle East and the Orient was a delightful experience for Albert and Elsa. Wherever they went, they saw architecture, costumes, landscapes that were unfamiliar to them. It was a remarkable experience, too. In city after city they were greeted by huge, friendly crowds that came to pay tribute—not to a great king or a victorious general—but to a simple man of science and of peace.

At each port of call, in Columbo, Singapore, Hong Kong, Shanghai, they were made welcome and were presented with many handsome gifts of teak and silk and ivory. When they landed in Japan, the day was declared a national holiday in Albert's honor.

For three months, they lived in Japan, part of the time in Tokyo, where Albert delivered lectures at the university. They went sight-seeing everywhere; to famous, snow-covered Mount Fuji, to Shinto and Buddhist religious shrines, on excursions through the countryside to see the carefully tended rice fields and the beautiful lakes and pine forests which are so numerous in Japan. They saw Japanese women wearing kimonos and wooden sandals, and they heard Japanese music played on the *samisen,* music that sounded odd but striking to Albert, whose ear was accustomed to the far different harmonies of his beloved Mozart.

More honors continued to come to him. In Tokyo, a telegram arrived, saying that he had been awarded the Nobel Prize in Physics. He didn't receive the prize for his work on relativity—that was still too "controversial"—but for the article on the "Quantum Theory of Light," which he had published in 1905, when he was still a clerk in the patent office in Berne. The prize money, fifty thousand dollars, he sent to Mileva in Switzerland, for her own use and to take care of their two sons.

Finally, their three months' stay in Japan was over, and Albert and Elsa took another ship back to the West. On the way home they left the ship in Egypt and traveled to Jerusalem, where they were the guests of Sir Herbert Samuel, the English Governor of Palestine.

Albert was particularly anxious to see the country which had come to mean so much to him, and for whose welfare he had toiled so faithfully. He found many things that pleased him. Work was continuing rapidly on the buildings of the Hebrew University on Mount Scopus. Begun in 1918, it did not open officially until

1925, but Albert delivered a special lecture on relativity there, the first lecture in the university's history.

He was also highly pleased by a trip that he made to the modern Jewish city of Tel Aviv. He saw spacious, clean apartment houses, wide, tree-lined streets, sunny, well-planned schools.

Best of all, he saw that Jews were filling all sorts of jobs, were engaged in an endless variety of occupations. This, Albert felt, was a great improvement on the way that so many Jews were forced to live in Europe. In Europe, because of restrictions against them, they often worked at the kinds of jobs that brought them only shame, the kinds of jobs that were "too disgusting" for anyone else to perform.

Albert was impressed by the new world that was being born in Palestine, and later he said of his visit, "I don't think I shall ever forget the sincerity and warmth of my reception . . . for they were to me an indication of the harmony and healthiness which reigns in the Jewish life in Palestine."

While Albert and Elsa were in Jerusalem, they received an invitation to come to Spain to visit the University of Madrid. Although they wanted to return home, conditions in Germany were still very unsettled. Inflation was raging, there was a dispute and open bloodshed with France, and the threat of a Nazi uprising. So Albert agreed to stay out of Germany for a while longer, and to go to Spain instead.

Once again, Albert and Elsa were graciously received; they had a private audience with King Alphonso XIII, and Albert was elected a member of the Spanish Academy of Science. He and Elsa were offered a house in Spain, where they could live in comfort, should conditions ever become "too unpleasant" for them in Germany. It was sad, Albert thought, that he was welcome in almost every country in the world except his own.

Another thought crossed his mind. How, as a boy of sixteen, dreaming of the day when there would be no more national boundaries, he had renounced his German citizenship to become something finer—a citizen of the world.

Now, by a fantastic turn of fortune, wasn't that actually what he had become? In France, England, America, China, Spain, he had been greeted by millions of plain people, not because he was a German professor who had worked for the glory of Germany, but because he was a scientist who had given his ideas freely to the world, for the benefit of men of all races and creeds. Truly, he had become a citizen of the world, in a way that he had never imagined possible.

At last their "grand tour" was over, and Albert and Elsa returned to Berlin. On the surface, at least, things were a little better in Germany now. Times were not quite so hard as they had been. Inflation was being controlled. There had been no new outbreak of Nazi terror.

Gradually, as the months passed, Elsa lost much of her fear that Albert would be harmed. As long as conditions were improving, she thought, life in Berlin was at least endurable.

But Albert was not deceived about the real state of Germany. Although the republican government seemed to be gaining strength, he believed that this was only a temporary illusion. Few Germans really felt loyalty to the Weimar Republic. In their hearts, they wanted a strong, nationalistic government, ruled by another emperor or by a dictator with absolute power, a man of blood and war.

Loyalty to the only liberal government that Germany had ever known kept Albert in Berlin long after his own reasoning told him that it would be wise to leave. Loyalty to his work kept him there, too. Among his colleagues at the Prussian Academy were many talented men, and his work often was helped by their knowledge and their opinions.

So Albert and Elsa remained in their apartment at 5 Haberlandstrasse, while the years began to slip away. Their home life was unchanged until Ilse, the elder of Albert's stepdaughters, married and moved to a home of her own. Then they were a household of three, Albert and Elsa and Albert's other stepdaughter, Margot.

Albert was often out of the country, traveling to scientific meetings in Belgium, Holland, France, and England; he also went to Geneva, where he served as a member of the League of Nations' Committee of Intellectual Cooperation. He had several friends on the Committee, Madame Curie, the discoverer of radium, Dr. Robert Millikan of the California Institute of Technology, and Professor Hendrik Lorenz of Holland, the man who had recognized the importance of Albert's work from his reading of the 1905 *Yearbook of Physics.*

At first Albert had held great hopes for the League of Nations and had accepted a position on the Committee in order to support the League's efforts to create a world of international justice and peace. But the League, Albert saw, was failing in its aims. He soon grew discouraged with committee meetings and spent less and less time attending them.

In Berlin, his schedule was busier than ever. He had his own work, and he devoted many of his free hours to helping others. He wrote letters of recommendation for talented and deserving people who needed jobs. He played in public concerts, to attract attention to young musicians, or to raise money to be sent to Palestine. He went to dinners, where he knew that his mere presence would increase contributions.

As a relief from his work, he had two hobbies which were very dear to him. He played his violin, sometimes alone, sometimes with a few friends who were equally skilled musicians. And during the summers, when the weather was fine, he sailed a little boat around the lakes and rivers that stretched beyond the outskirts of the city.

Other sailboat owners grew accustomed to seeing him there, his pipe between his teeth, his long hair blowing in the wind, a smile of contentment on his face, as he steered his boat through the sparkling waters.

As the years passed, fame meant less and less to Albert. It always had made him uncomfortable. He believed that public worship of any individual was a grave mistake, and in his own case, he felt that his great reputation was undeserved, that a dozen other scientists should have shared it with him.

He found it difficult, at times, even to think of himself as "the famous Dr. Einstein." It was as though he had become two people, his private self, and his public personality. Once he wrote a letter to George Bernard Shaw, thanking Shaw for compliments "addressed to my mythical namesake, who makes my life a singular burden."

When something happened that showed how famous he was, Albert remained unimpressed. Once, two American students made a bet, whether or not a letter addressed to "Professor Albert Einstein, Europe," would reach its proper destination. When Albert received the letter—it arrived without delay—he said nothing except, "How excellent the postal service is."

Nor was he willing to dress the part of a famous man. Elsa always had a terrible struggle to get him into evening clothes when they went to a banquet. And from time to time, she had to steal the oldest of his suits and give it away because it was too threadbare for him to wear in public.

His favorite costume was a heavy sweater, worn without a shirt or necktie, old trousers, and sneakers that were loose and comfortable. He said that attention to dress was a waste of time—and one day he proudly announced to an old friend of Elsa's, Antonina Vallentin, that he had given up wearing socks.

"I've discovered," he said, "that one can easily wear shoes without socks—socks, you know, get holes in them—my wife does nothing but mend them. I'll never wear them again, now that I can do without them."

Albert, though he often found fame a burden, was also aware that he had been very fortunate in his career. In 1926, when the Royal Society of London presented him with the Copley Medal, its highest award, he expressed these feelings about his life and work: "The man who has discovered an idea which allows us to penetrate, to whatever slight degree, a little more deeply the eternal mystery of nature, has been allotted a great share of grace. If, in addition, he experiences the best help, sympathy and recognition of his time, he attains almost more happiness than one man can bear."

On a trip to Switzerland in 1928, Albert suffered his first serious illness since the war. He tried to move a heavy trunk, the strain was too great for him, and it brought on a heart attack.

For several weeks, he was near death. Then, little by
little, he began to grow stronger, and finally, when he
was well enough, he was put on the train and taken back
home to Berlin.

He was forced to give up all work, all exercise, all
amusements, for several months. He wasn't allowed tobacco and he had to eat carefully. Elsa was terrified at
first, but she quickly mastered her fears and took charge
of his care, assisted by Margot. By the spring of the next
year, the doctors said that Albert had completely recovered, and would suffer no further attacks if he avoided
overexertion.

In 1929 he published a new work, the "Unified Field
Theory." In this theory, he attempted to discover a single law governing both gravitation and electromagnet-
ism, the two fundamental forces of the universe. This
first attempt, Albert said later, was unsuccessful; but it
marked a new direction for his work, and he spent the
rest of his life following it.

Albert also celebrated his fiftieth birthday in 1929.
Presents arrived from all over the world, and so many
letters and telegrams came each day that they had to be
brought inside the Einstein apartment in bushel baskets.
Friends stopped by to help Elsa unwrap the presents,
but they did not see Albert. He had gone into hiding in
the country to avoid the excitement, and only Elsa and
Margot knew where he was.

Then Berlin decided to honor its most famous citizen

on his fiftieth birthday. Knowing how fond Albert was of small boats, the City Council offered to give him a summer villa on the shores of a nearby river, so that all summer long he could go sailing whenever he pleased.

German newspapers proudly printed the story of the city's generosity—until the Council discovered that it couldn't give the villa to Albert. Another family was already living in it and refused to move out.

A new plan was made. Albert would be given some land which the city owned, near the villa, and then the Einsteins could build a house of their own design. So, Albert and Elsa picked a site which they liked—and the City Council found that it didn't have the power to give the land away either.

Its embarrassment growing, the Council decided on a third plan. Albert and Elsa were to pick out any site they liked for a summer home, and the city would buy the land for them. Albert and Elsa found such a site at Caputh, a suburb, about an hour's train ride from the city.

But when the Council met to grant the money it had promised, several Nazi members of the Council raised objections. Why should such a gift be given by the city? Did Einstein really deserve it? What authority did the Council have for giving away the money of the people? A bitter debate followed. The Council couldn't reach a decision and the promised money was not voted.

When Albert was told of this, he lost his temper, and

wrote a letter to the Mayor of Berlin, in which he said, "My dear Mr. Mayor: Human life is very short, while the authorities work very slowly. I feel therefore that my life is too short for me to adapt myself to your methods. I thank you for your friendly intentions. Now, however, my birthday is past and I decline the gift."

Albert decided to take matters into his own hands. He and Elsa already had spent so much time with the architects, planning the kind of house they wanted, and so much time finding exactly the right place to build it, that he said they would build it themselves, and pay for the land too, out of their own money.

A short while later, when Professor Philipp Frank was in Berlin, Elsa said to him, "In this way, without wanting it, we have acquired a beautiful home of our own situated in the woods near the water. But we have also spent most of our savings. Now we have no money, but we have our land and our property. This gives one a much greater sense of security."

Albert did not share his wife's feelings in the matter. He had told Professor Frank, in 1921, that he would not care to live in Germany in ten years' time—and those ten years were almost up now.

Nineteen twenty-nine was a fateful year in history. In October, a world-wide depression began, and before many months had passed, times were very hard in Germany again. Businesses failed, factories were shut down, millions of workers were thrown out of their jobs. Soon there were breadlines, and poverty, and hunger, and the specter of revolution.

In the 1930 elections, the Nazi Party received more than six million votes out of a total of thirty-five million cast. In the next election, they won 230 seats out of 607, and became the largest party in the Reichstag, Germany's congress.

Thousands of young men, despairing of the future, turned to the new German leader, Adolf Hitler. He offered them food, jobs, and "a glorious new era for the Fatherland." In exchange, they had only to give up their personal freedom, and agree to obey the will of the state. The Weimar Republic, so fragile from the beginning, began to totter and sink.

In 1930, and again in 1931, Albert spent the winter months in Pasadena, as visiting professor at the California Institute of Technology. He returned to Berlin early in 1932, just in time to watch the presidential election in March.

The two leading candidates were Hitler, and the hero of World War I, now more than eighty years old, General Paul von Hindenburg. Von Hindenburg was supported by the German liberals, and he won the election. But he was hardly in office when he betrayed them by appointing Franz von Papen to the all-important office of Chancellor.

Von Papen was determined to crush democracy in Germany, and he set about doing it with the help of the Army. For a time, some people thought that Von Papen and the Army would keep Hitler from becoming Chancellor and gaining complete power over the country. Albert did not share this view. At his summer home in Caputh, in the summer of 1932, he told his friend Professor Frank, "I am convinced that a military regime will not prevent the imminent National Socialist Revolution."

During that summer, a famous American educator, Dr. Abraham Flexner, a man who had done great pioneer work in improving medical schools in America, came to Berlin especially to see Albert. Two years before, in 1930, Dr. Flexner had encouraged Mr. Louis Bamberger and his sister, Mrs. Felix Fuld, to donate five million dollars to found the Institute for Advanced Study in Princeton.

Dr. Flexner had met Albert several times in America. Now he asked Albert if he would be interested in becoming one of the Institute's first members? He would not have to lecture, he would have no specific duties, he could work on his theories when and how he pleased, and he would have valuable colleagues at Princeton and all the assistants he could use.

Albert thought of his visit to Princeton in 1921, the pretty, old-fashioned New Jersey town, the quiet streets, the cherry trees in blossom—yes, it would be a pleasant place to work and live, a peaceful place in which to close out one's life.

"For the time being," he said to Dr. Flexner, "I am still under obligation to spend the coming winter in Pasadena. Later, however, I shall be ready to work for you."

In the autumn of 1932, Albert and Elsa were scheduled to leave Germany again for California. Standing in front of their house in Caputh, Albert said, "Before you leave this time, take a good look at your house."

"Why?" Elsa said.

"You will never see it again," he told her.

In less than six months, while they were in Pasadena in January, President von Hindenburg appointed a new Chancellor for Germany—Adolf Hitler.

14

When they left for Europe in the early spring of 1933, Albert and Elsa did not return to their Berlin apartment. Instead, they made arrangements to rent a house in the little Belgian seaside resort of Le-Coq-Sur-Mer.

The Nazis had already begun their campaign to destroy the Jews in Germany, and Albert became the object of their most vicious libels. He was the secret leader, they said, of a vast conspiracy to betray the German people and to overthrow the government.

While still at sea, he and Elsa received word that the police, searching for "hidden weapons and ammunition," had ransacked their summer home in Caputh. A bread knife had been found in the kitchen, and was being displayed by the Nazis as "proof" of how dangerous Professor Einstein really was.

Albert and Elsa were relieved to learn, on their arrival in Europe, that both Margot and Ilse had managed to escape from Germany. Soon Margot joined them, and

with Helen Dukas, Albert's secretary, they moved into
the house in Le-Coq-Sur-Mer.

Albert was now faced with a disagreeable problem.
He was still a member of the Prussian Academy. The
Nazis wanted him to be dismissed, but Albert was sure
that his old friend, Max Planck, one of the two scientists
who had brought him to Berlin in 1913, would not wish
this to happen. On the other hand, if the Academy did
nothing, and allowed Albert to remain a member, the
Nazis might make a great deal of trouble for Max
Planck. To save his friend from the anger of the Nazis,
Albert decided to resign from the Academy, ending
twenty years of the closest ties with his German colleagues.

During the spring and summer, the Nazis increased
their anti-Semitic persecutions. Jewish professors were
fired from their jobs. Jewish doctors were forbidden to
practice in hospitals. Jewish lawyers were barred from
the courts. Albert could no longer be hurt in this way,
but he still owned property in Germany. The Nazis
confiscated his summer home, his bank account, and the
personal possessions which they found in the apartment
at 5 Haberlandstrasse.

Le-Coq-Sur-Mer was not far from the German border. Although Albert insisted that he was in no danger,
Elsa was frightened at the thought that a Nazi assassin
might easily slip into Belgium and try to kill him.

She was not alone in her fears. The King and Queen

of Belgium, who had been friends of Albert for many years, realized his danger and had his house surrounded by secret service men. Two of them were appointed his bodyguards and followed him whenever he left the house, whether he liked it or not.

Albert was invited to stay in England, where he would be safer than in Belgium, but at first he refused to go. Then, a rumor began to circulate that the Nazis had offered a reward of a thousand English pounds—about five thousand dollars—for the murder of "the traitor Einstein."

On being told of this, Albert said, "I never knew that I was worth so much"—but he saw how terrified Elsa had become, and he finally agreed to flee to England.

On a dark, summer night, Elsa, Margot, Helen Dukas and Albert were led to a waiting car, driven to a secret port, and placed on a ship that carried them across the English Channel. Then they were taken to London, and from there, to a country house in Norfolk, overlooking the sea, where they were heavily guarded by English secret service men until the time came for them to sail to America.

In October they arrived safely in Princeton and moved into the house at 2 Library Place which had been provided for them. Five thousand miles separated them from Berlin, and for the first time in months, Elsa could breathe easily again.

Albert began to work at the Institute for Advanced Study, and after a few weeks in Princeton, already thought of America as his permanent home. Because he had traveled so widely during his life, and because he had few conventional feelings of patriotism, he knew little of the unhappiness that most men feel when they are exiled from their native country.

Many sorrows, though, darkened his declining years. Death became a familiar occurrence, claiming most of those who were dearest to him. Paul Langevin of France, Hendrik Lorenz, Madame Curie, his oldest scientific friends—at times, the number of vanished faces seemed without end.

In 1934 Elsa was summoned to Paris, where her daughter Ilse had fallen ill. She arrived only in time to witness Ilse's death, and when she returned to Princeton her own health was badly impaired.

Elsa never fully recovered from the shock of losing her daughter. Two years later, just after moving into their new house on Mercer Street, her strength began to fail. The doctors were unable to stop the course of her disease and in a short time, she too was dead.

Albert's friends were dismayed at the change that came over him. His face grew ashen and seemed to take on new wrinkles, his shoulders slumped, his gait became slower—as though, in losing Elsa, the person closest to his heart, he had become an old man in the space of a few days.

Other sorrows weighed down his spirits, as the months and the years passed. He learned of relatives and friends who were forced to flee from Germany to escape the Nazis, often with nothing more than the clothes on their backs. He learned of certain professors, many of them old scientific colleagues, who couldn't bear the thought of beginning life in a new country, and who killed themselves in their misery and despair.

Many Jewish refugees wrote to Albert, and came to his house in Princeton to ask for help. They believed him to be far more influential than he really was, but he did what he could to find them jobs, to give them clothes or money, to hold out a hand to those who had nothing. He played his violin at charity concerts, he sat for his portrait, he wrote letters of recommendation—and was criticized for using his name too often and weakening the effect of his great reputation.

He was also criticized for stating publicly that he was no longer a pacifist. Hitler had to be stopped, and if necessary, stopped by force of arms. How, his critics asked, could Dr. Einstein turn his back on the principles he had held all his life?

His answer was clear: conditions in the world had changed since the advent of Hitler and the Nazis. In 1914 Germany had wanted to dominate Europe, not to destroy it. In 1914 war was wrong because it was unnecessary, and because, no matter which side won, all the peoples of Europe would be losers. In 1938 war was right, because Hitler would be satisfied with nothing less than the conquest of Europe, and because, if the peoples of Europe refused to defend themselves, they would lose freedom, happiness, even life itself. Surely, to fight for these things, to defend one's country and one's family against enslavement and perhaps extinction could not be wrong.

This was hardly a popular view to hold in the late 1930's. Many Americans and Europeans had convinced themselves that Hitler was not a madman, hungry for world power, and that stories of Germany's anti-Semitism, of the beatings, humiliations, and murders in Nazi concentration camps were greatly exaggerated.

"Now that Hitler," these people said, "has annexed Austria, now that the German part of Czechoslovakia has been given to him, there will be no further trouble. Hitler will prove to be a reasonable man. He will be satisfied and we will have 'peace in our time.' "

Albert was certain that England and France, and eventually the United States, would be forced to fight a war with Germany, and he greatly feared that in their present state of disarmament they would not be strong enough to win that war.

Then, one morning at the end of July 1939, two Hungarian physicists, Dr. Leo Szilard of Columbia University and Dr. Eugene Wigner of Princeton, came to Albert's house with the story of a recent scientific discovery that could change the very nature of war itself.

The story began months before, in Berlin, at the Kaiser Wilhelm Institute. During a series of experiments, two German physicists, Otto Hahn and Lise Meitner, had made a puzzling discovery. They had bombarded a quantity of uranium with neutrons—and the uranium had released a tremendous amount of energy.

Before the full significance of their discovery was realized, the Nazis declared that Lise Meitner was a "non-Aryan," and she fled the country, taking with her the notes from her experiments. In Stockholm, where she was safe, she repeated these experiments, with the same amazing result. She knew then how important the discovery was, and she wrote of her findings to another physicist, Dr. O. R. Frisch, who was at the University of Copenhagen.

Dr. Frisch repeated the experiments, and exactly the same effect was produced a third time. He and Lise Meitner coined a phrase for the phenomenon—"nuclear fission."

Word of nuclear fission spread quickly through the scientific world. Dr. Frisch wrote to Niels Bohr, a famous physicist and Nobel Prize winner. Dr. Bohr was in America just then. He showed the work of Dr. Frisch and Lise Meitner to Enrico Fermi, an Italian, who had fled from fascist Italy and was now a teacher at Columbia University.

Dr. Fermi and his colleague, Dr. Szilard, conducted new experiments during the early months of 1939. They proved that it was possible to control a nuclear reaction which meant, theoretically at least, that an atomic bomb could be built whose destructive power would dwarf any other man-made force in the world.

Dr. Fermi and Dr. Szilard also heard an alarming report from Berlin. At the Kaiser Wilhelm Institute, Otto Hahn had been put in charge of a team of two hundred German scientists, to make further experiments with uranium. Clearly their object was to discover how to make an atomic bomb and to place it at the disposal of the Nazis.

This was the story that Dr. Szilard and Dr. Wigner told Albert in the cluttered study at 112 Mercer Street. Albert examined the notes they had brought, and understood at once the significance of what had happened— and where the chain of events had begun.

Almost thirty-five years before, he had set a formula down on paper—$E=MC^2$—and here was the dramatic proof, both of the tremendous forces within the atom, and of the fact that man was on the threshold of releasing those forces, either for his own good, or for his own destruction.

But why, Albert asked his visitors, had they come to see him? He was not an atomic physicist. He could be of very little help in their future experiments.

They needed his help in another way, they said. If it

were possible to build an atomic bomb, America had to build it first, before Germany did. The safety, perhaps the survival of the civilized world might depend on it.

The difficulty was that only a highly trained scientist could appreciate the meaning of Lise Meitner's discovery. Untrained persons—the President of the United States himself—might think that "nuclear fission" was just a laboratory theory without practical value—unless the subject was brought to his attention by a scientist whose reputation he already knew and respected.

Dr. Szilard and Dr. Wigner looked at Albert. Would he write to President Roosevelt, and present the facts?

It was perhaps the most ironic moment in Albert's life. From earliest childhood he had hated soldiers, uniforms, war, the idea of one man killing another. And now he was being asked to help in the development of the most destructive military weapon ever dreamed of by man—a weapon that could kill hundreds of thousands of people in less than a second.

Yet if he refused to write to the President, and if America did not build an atomic bomb, would that stop the experiments at the Kaiser Wilhelm Institute? If Hitler gained possession of such a bomb, would there be any way to prevent his conquest of Europe, Asia, America?

When he was alone again, Albert sat down wearily at his desk. Finally he picked up his pen, and wrote this letter to President Roosevelt:

2 August, 1939

Sir:

Some recent work by E. Fermi and L. Szilard, which has been communicated to me in manuscript, leads me to expect that the element Uranium may be turned into a new and important source of energy in the immediate future. . . .

. . . it may become possible to set up a nuclear chain reaction in a large mass of Uranium. . . .

This new phenomenon would also lead to the construction of bombs, and it is conceivable—though much less certain—that extremely powerful bombs of a new type may thus be constructed. A single bomb of this type, carried by a boat and exploded in a port, might very well destroy the whole port together with some of the surrounding territory. . . .

Yours very truly,

A. Einstein

When the President received Albert's letter, he and his advisers recognized the importance of what it said. Almost at once, with full government support, a number of scientists were gathered together, and work began on the "Manhattan Project," work which finally led to the construction of America's atomic bomb.

And less than a month after Albert's letter was written to President Roosevelt, the armies of Nazi Germany stormed across the borders of Poland, and World War II had finally begun.

15

During the war and the years of peace that followed, Albert remained in Princeton, living a retired life in the white frame house at 112 Mercer Street. Margot lived there, too, as did Helen Dukas. From 1939, until her death, Albert's sister, Maya, also lived in the Mercer Street house, and the three women helped to fill the void in Albert's life which had been created by the death of his beloved Elsa.

Albert taught a few young scientists at the Institute for Advanced Study, and continued to work on his own ideas. Until the very end of his life, he devoted himself to completing the "Unified Field Theory."

Even today, there is still no agreement on the Unified Field Theory. Some scientists believe that Albert's greatest achievement was the earlier General Theory of Relativity. Others are not sure—they believe that it will be many years before anyone can prove or disprove the complicated equations that Albert finally evolved toward the end of his life.

In common with other scientists, Albert was sickened by the horrors of atomic warfare, the awful explosions over Nagasaki and Hiroshima, and the responsible part that they themselves had played in building the most destructive weapon in history. Shortly after the war, Albert made a speech in New York, in which he described his feelings, and his concern for the future.

"Today," he said, "the physicists who participated in forging the most formidable and dangerous weapon of all times are harassed by an equal feeling of responsibility, not to say guilt. And we cannot desist from warning, and warning again, we cannot slacken in our efforts to make the nations of the world, and especially their governments, aware of the unspeakable disaster they are certain to provoke, unless they change their attitude toward each other and toward the task of shaping the future. . . . The war is won, but the peace is not."

On another occasion, he offered his ideas for building a peaceful world. "The release of atomic energy," he said, "has not created a new problem. It has merely made more urgent the necessity of solving an existing one. . . . So long as there are sovereign nations possessing great power, war is inevitable. . . .

"I do not believe that the secret of the bomb should be given to the United Nations Organization. I do not believe that it should be given to the Soviet Union. . . .

The secret of the bomb should be committed to a world government, and the United States should immediately announce its readiness to give it to a world government. This government should be founded by the United States, the Soviet Union, and Great Britain, the only three powers with great military strength."

The passage of time has proved the wisdom of many of Albert's political ideas. Though the United States, Great Britain, and the Soviet Union have certainly not founded a world government, they have come to agree that control of the atomic and hydrogen bomb is a first step toward international peace, and that peace today is the most serious problem that mankind has ever faced. Because of this agreement between the three major powers, there is hope at last that war itself may eventually be outlawed, and that all nations, despite their internal differences, may learn to work together for their mutual benefit.

Whatever disappointment Albert may have felt at the time, when he saw how slowly some of his ideas were accepted, he must have drawn satisfaction from the efforts he had previously made on behalf of the Zionist movement, and from the success of the Jews in Palestine, who declared themselves a sovereign people in 1948, and established the new nation of Israel.

Auschwitz, Buchenwald, Dachau—Hitler's concentration camps—had completed the tragedy of the Jews in Europe; but for the survivors, and for oppressed Jews everywhere, there was now a land of refuge where they would be made welcome, and where they could take the first steps toward a new, a decent, a happy life.

Nor were Albert's efforts on behalf of Zionism forgotten by the people of Israel. When Chaim Weizmann, the nation's first president, died in 1952, the presidency was offered to Albert. He declined the honor, for he knew that he could never suitably fill the position of political leader. But of all the honors he received in his life, this gesture by the Jews of Israel must have touched him most deeply.

The passing years had left his mind unimpaired; in 1953, at the age of seventy-four, he announced that he had finally completed work on the Unified Field Theory. But his body had grown steadily weaker, and one day, just a year later, newspapers and radios carried the news around the world that Albert Einstein had died in Princeton, after a brief illness.

To scientists, in their special world, Albert had been a titan who left behind a record of great accomplishments. To the unscientific, he had been a man of almost magical wisdom, and a gentle man of peace. To the Jews of the world, he had been an inspiring leader during one of the most tragic episodes in Jewish history.

Many words were written about Albert after his death, and many attempts were made to explain his personal philosophy. Yet perhaps the most revealing words of all were those that he had once set down himself, when he said, "Only a life lived for others is a life worthwhile."

In his efforts to understand the nature of the universe, to promote peace between nations, to protect the rights of all men, Jew and gentile, from the brutal forces of oppression—in the efforts of a lifetime—he had been completely selfless, and the peoples of the world, perceiving this, mourned his death.

Covenant Books

Stories of Jewish Men and Women
To Inspire and Instruct Young People

Covenant Books are a new and fascinating series designed to take young people, eleven to fifteen years of age, on an adventurous expedition into the realms of Jewish experience. This is achieved by means of colorful biographies of Jewish personalities—prophets, rabbis, martyrs, philanthropists, writers, scientists—each representative of the many facets of a great tradition.

Covenant Books Already Published

1 SILVERSMITH OF OLD NEW YORK: MYER MYERS *by William Wise*

2 BORDER HAWK: AUGUST BONDI *by Lloyd Alexander*

3 THE WORLD OF JO DAVIDSON *by Lois Harris Kuhn*

4 JUBAL AND THE PROPHET *by Frieda Clark Hyman*

5 THE UNCOMMON SOLDIER: THE STORY OF MAJOR ALFRED MORDECAI *by Robert D. Abrahams*

6 LIBERTY'S DAUGHTER: THE STORY OF EMMA LAZARUS *by Eve Merriam*

7 KEYS TO A MAGIC DOOR: ISAAC LEIB PERETZ *by Sylvia Rothchild*

8 ABOAB: THE FIRST RABBI OF THE AMERICAS *by Emily Hahn*

9 NORTHWEST PIONEER: THE STORY OF LOUIS FLEISCHNER *by Alfred Apsler*

10 ALBERT EINSTEIN: CITIZEN OF THE WORLD *by William Wise*

$$\frac{x^2}{y^2} - dy^2 - dx^2$$

$$\left. \frac{m \, u_i}{\sqrt{1-u^2}} \right)$$

$$+ \frac{1}{2} m u^2, \; m \, u_i \biggr)$$

$$\left| \; \frac{m \, u_i}{\sqrt{1-u^2}} \; Impuls \right.$$

$$m \left(\frac{1}{\sqrt{1-u^2}} - 1 \right) Kin \, Ene$$

$$\frac{t' + v x'}{\sqrt{1-v^2}} \; \left| \; x = \frac{x' + v t'}{\sqrt{1-v^2}} \; y = y' \; z = z \right.$$